To my dad, Charlie, my late mum, Mary, husband Claudio and children Charlotte and Rowan. You are my inspiration and always keep me smiling.

Contents

2 Bread, Pizzas and Calzones

5 Sauces and Pesto

8 Sides

9 Desserts, Cakes, Biscuits and Drinks

Acknowledgements

Thank you to my dad, Charlie, my husband, Claudio, and my two children, Charlotte and Rowan, who were most patient with me as I researched and wrote this book. The up side is that you did get to try all the recipes as I tested them, but maybe I should have spread it out over a year!

Thank you to all my colleagues here at Ballyknocken House and Cookery School, especially Sharon, Mary, Gema, Rowena, Aoife and Ruth. I am truly grateful for your commitment and great humour. Thanks to Aileen O'Brien for your hard work, dedication and encouragement.

A special thanks to Claudio's family, especially Zia Lina, Antonio and Bruna, Francesco and Ornella, Rosamaria and Toti, Antonella and Reno and their families for welcoming me so warmly. To Solina and her family and Franco Cucuru and his family for sharing your food passion with me. To Armando for helping me to master the Italian language. To Lorenzo for keeping your eye on my lemons – without you, there would be no limoncello.

Thank you to Colm, Rory, Sonya, Peter, Barry, Brendan, Declan, Niall, Aldo and the wonderful team at RTÉ Cork who worked on the TV series. Thank you especially to Rory for your exceptional photography on location.

To Conor, Adam and all at Roma for your wonderful support. And finally, thanks to Hugh, Orla, Jo, Fergal, Nicki, Aoife, Kristin, Teresa and all of the Gill & Macmillan team for your fantastic guidance and belief.

Grazie mille,
Catherine

Introduction

My husband Claudio's family says that 'cooking shows off the skill of the cook, but Italian cooking shows off the skill of God'. It's all about the best of what nature provides.

And funnily, that's where my story starts. I was brought up on a traditional Irish farm, with parents who valued the importance of producing and growing our own ingredients. My mother was not only a committed foodie, but she also developed a business on her passion. I got my foundation in cooking from hanging onto her apron strings, cooking three meals a day for our guesthouse residents, making butter, helping milk the cows, harvesting fruit and vegetables and baking for the local country market. So years later, when I found myself locked into a pub in Dublin chatting to a Sicilian man, Claudio Fulvio, also a foodie, my fate was sealed.

As the years went on, we immersed ourselves in Italian food culture. Back on our farm in Wicklow, we also opened our cookery school and at the same time continued with our farming, cooking and guesthouse businesses. Along came our two gorgeous (well, I would say that!) children.

We have a base in Sicily too and relish every moment spent there in the company of our local friends and family, harvesting our lemons, oranges, mulberries and olives, shopping at the markets, cooking together and always learning.

I see Italian cooking through Irish eyes and this book is a reflection of that. Sometimes I amuse Claudio's cousins as I try to take a shortcut in a recipe or substitute an ingredient. They are at pains to try to teach me the 'rules' of Italian cooking.

I always smile at the rules – in a country where you can drink alcohol at any age, there are hundreds of unwritten rules of food and cooking in Italy. Here's a taster:

* The ingredients must be fresh and in season, which is understandable.

* If the recipe is perfected, absolutely don't change it.

* No garlic and onions together when making tomato sauce.

* No garlic with fish unless in fish soup (*zuppe*).

* No olive oil (extra virgin, of course) in the pasta cooking water unless it's fresh pasta.

* Always add the pasta to the sauce, never the sauce to the pasta.

* Never use a spoon with your pasta unless it's *in brodo* (in broth).

* Never cut your spaghetti, not even if you are three years old.

* No Parmesan with fish, unless it's *spaghetti al nero di sepia* (spaghetti with squid ink).

* No cappuccino after 12 o'clock, unless you're a tourist.

* It's caffé, not espresso, otherwise you are clearly a blow-in.

* It's OK to eat ice cream for breakfast!

* And most importantly, listen to your mama, she knows best.

Finally, there's the old saying, *'Chi la sera i pasti li ha fatti, sta agli altri lavare i piatti'* ('If one cooks the meal, then the others wash up'). Now there's a rule that's often broken.

Buon appetito!
Catherine

Note on Ingredients

Flour

The two main types of flour used in Italian baking and pasta making are *grano duro* and '00' flour.

Durum wheat (*grano duro*) can be milled reasonably finely and is characterised by its yellow colour and grainy texture. It's often referred to as semolina flour in this part of the world. This flour is perfect for making pasta, especially long pasta.

Italian '00' flour (*Dopio Zero*) is double refined to give a very silky, smooth, powdery flour and is usually from the *grano tenero* grain. This flour is ideal for breads, cakes, pastries and pizzas. An alternative to this, but not an exact match, is strong white flour, also known as bread or baker's flour.

Olive Oil

I use very high-quality extra virgin olive oil (which contains no more than 0.8% acidity) for salad dressings, herb oils, adding at the table to soups and stews and for drizzling. For frying and general cooking, I use a medium-range extra virgin olive oil.

Tomatoes

If you can't get lovely, ripe, juicy tomatoes, use good-quality tinned plum Italian tomatoes instead. Sicilian Pachino tomatoes are tastier and sweeter than any other variety – the constant dry and sunny climate is ideal for the production of this crop.

Note on Symbols

Recipes that are easy to prepare have an **E** symbol.

Recipes that can be frozen have the **F** symbol.

Conversion Charts

All oven temperatures in the book are for a conventional oven. For a fan oven, reduce the temperature by 15–20%, depending on your oven. Below are approximate equivalents. In any recipe, use either metric or imperial measurements: never mix the two.

WEIGHT

30 g	1 oz
60 g	2 oz
90 g	3 oz
110 g	4 oz
140 g	5 oz
170 g	6 oz
200 g	7 oz
225 g	8 oz
250 g	9 oz
280 g	10 oz
350 g	12 oz
310 g	11 oz
340 g	12 oz
370 g	13 oz
400 g	14 oz
425 g	15 oz
450 g	1 lb

VOLUME

5 ml	1 tsp
15 ml	1 tbsp
30 ml	1 fl oz
60 ml	2 fl oz
90 ml	3 fl oz
120 ml	4 fl oz
150 ml	5 fl oz
175 ml	6 fl oz
200 ml	7 fl oz
240 ml	8 fl oz
270 ml	9 fl oz
300 ml	10 fl oz
325 ml	11 fl oz
350 ml	12 fl oz
400 ml	14 fl oz
450 ml	15 fl oz
475 ml	16 fl oz
1 litre	34 fl oz

OVEN

Degrees Celsius	Degrees Fahrenheit	Gas Mark	Description
140	275	1	very cool
150	300	2	cool
160	325	3	warm
180	350	4	moderate
190	375	5	fairly hot
200	400	6	fairly hot
220	425	7	hot
230	450	8	very hot
240	475	9	very hot

Antipasta, Starters and Salads

Beef Carpaccio
Carpaccio di manzo

Marinated Aubergine with Goat's Cheese and Herbs
Melanzane marinate con caprino e erbe

Caponata

Stuffed Rice Balls
Arancini di riso

Marinated Peppers
Peperoni marinati

Aubergine Parmigiana
Melanzane alla Parmigiana

Roasted Stuffed Peppers
Peperoni ripieni al forno

Marinated Olives
Olive marinate

Grilled Portobello Mushrooms with Lemon and Rosemary Oil
Funghi portobello alla griglia con limone e olio al rosmarino

Chickpea Fritters
Panelle

Stuffed and Fried Courgette Blossoms
Fiori di zucca fritti e ripieni

Crunchy Vegetables with Warm Anchovy Sauce
Bagna cauda

Tuscan Bread Salad
Panzanella

Courgette and Thyme Frittata
Frittata di zucchine e timo

Caprese Salad
Insalata Caprese

Seared Scallops with Fennel Salad and Orange Basil Dressing
*Cappesante ai ferri con insalata di finocchi e salsa all'arancia
e basilica*

Crostini, Bruschetta and Fettunta

Tomato and Caper Crostini
Crostini ai pomodori e capperi

Goat's Cheese and Chive Crostini
Crostini ai formaggio di capra e erba

Chicken Liver Crostini
Crostini al fegato di pollo

Prosciutto, Pesto, Walnut and Fig Bruschetta
Bruschetta con prosciutto, pesto, noci e fichi

Mushroom, Parmesan and Truffle Oil Bruschetta
Bruschetta ai funghi, Parmigiano e olio al tartufo

Tomato Fettunta
Fettunta al pomodoro

Beef Carpaccio

Carpaccio di manzo

Serves 6

Of all the delicious things to come out of Harry's Bar in Venice, including the Bellini cocktail, carpaccio tops the list for me. Generally, carpaccio refers to very thinly sliced raw beef, but nowadays the term is widely used, from swordfish carpaccio to pineapple.

300g fillet steak, cut into wafer-thin slices
extra virgin olive oil
1 tbsp lemon juice
salt and freshly ground black pepper
rocket, to garnish
Parmesan shavings

1. Spread the slices of steak on a serving platter. Drizzle with olive oil and the lemon juice. Season with salt and freshly ground black pepper.
2. Garnish with rocket, sprinkle over the Parmesan shavings and serve.

✱ It's possible to buy beef carpaccio precut and prepacked, but I always buy it fresh and ask my butcher to slice the beef. That way, I'm assured of freshness and provenance.

Marinated Aubergine with Goat's Cheese and Herbs

Melanzane marinate con caprino e erbe

Serves 4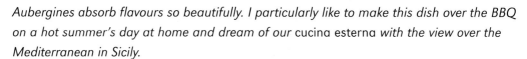

Aubergines absorb flavours so beautifully. I particularly like to make this dish over the BBQ on a hot summer's day at home and dream of our cucina esterna with the view over the Mediterranean in Sicily.

2 large aubergines, sliced lengthways into 2cm-thick slices
5 tbsp extra virgin olive oil, plus extra for vegetables
juice of 1 lemon
1 ½ tbsp finely chopped flat-leaf parsley
1 garlic clove, minced
salt and freshly ground black pepper
200g goat's cheese, crumbled
1 large sprig of thyme or oregano

1. Heat a skillet or frying pan (or BBQ) until very hot. Brush the aubergines with a little oil and fry in batches until soft and cooked through. Arrange on a platter.
2. Mix together the 5 tbsp olive oil, lemon juice, parsley, garlic and salt and pepper. Drizzle over the cooked aubergines. Let the flavours blend for 5 minutes, then scatter the goat's cheese and thyme over and serve.

✳ Try a little feta instead of the goat's cheese.

Caponata

Serves 6

It's impossible to leave the shores of Sicily without having sampled caponata at least once during your stay. It's on every antipasta menu, and if you're lucky enough to enjoy home dining, then every family has their own variation of the recipe – and everybody's mother makes the best caponata, or so they tell me. The recipe also varies according to the region of Sicily; for example, in the mountains you'll find potatoes added to it.

This is my version of the recipe, which I enjoy as an antipasta and also served as a side to fish (apologies to Zia Lina, I know the latter is not at all authentic!).

2 medium aubergines, cut into 2cm cubes
salt and freshly ground black pepper
extra virgin olive oil
2 large onions, chopped
5 celery stalks, trimmed and cut into 1.5cm pieces
500ml tomato sauce (p. 130)

65g capers, rinsed
50ml white wine vinegar
sugar, to taste
125g green olives
crusty bread, to serve

1. Degorge the aubergine by placing the cubes in a colander and sprinkling with salt. Leave for 30 minutes to allow the bitter juices to drain, then rinse the aubergine and pat dry.
2. Heat some olive oil in a deep frying pan. Shallow fry the aubergines until they are soft and golden in colour. Drain on kitchen paper.
3. Heat a pan with oil. Sauté the onions and celery on a low heat for 7–10 minutes, until they begin to colour. Add the tomato sauce, capers, vinegar and sugar and simmer for 5 minutes. Add the aubergine and olives and cook for a further 10 minutes. Season to taste with salt and freshly ground black pepper.
4. Allow to cool and refrigerate for 24 hours before serving. Serve at room temperature with crusty bread.

✳ For more of an Arab influence to this dish, add raisins and pine nuts.

*Marinated peppers (left),
stuffed rice balls (centre),
caponata (right)*

Stuffed Rice Balls

Arancini di riso

Makes 15 balls

Arancini are a huge favourite with my children. They are Sicilian stuffed rice balls, coated in breadcrumbs and deep fried, and are so called because they resemble oranges when cooked. The filling varies from region to region and can be anything from simple butter to ham and mozzarella. The recipe here is also a typical street food in Palermo.

pinch of saffron
600g Arborio rice (or other risotto rice)
1 tsp salt
olive oil
1 onion, finely chopped
250g lean minced beef
130g cooked peas
4 tbsp dry white wine

½ tsp finely chopped thyme
salt and freshly ground black pepper
3 large eggs, separated
50g freshly grated Parmesan
  (or Pecorino) cheese
100g flour, for dredging
150g breadcrumbs

1. Dissolve the saffron in 125ml warm water.
2. Place the rice in a saucepan with the saffron water and add another 1 ½ litres of water. Add the salt and bring to the boil. Cover, lower the heat and simmer until the water has been absorbed and the rice is tender, which will take about 20 minutes. Let the rice cool to room temperature.
3. Meanwhile, heat some olive oil in a large frying pan. Sauté the onion on a low heat for 7–10 minutes, until transparent. Add the minced beef and cook, stirring, for about 5 minutes, until the meat is fully cooked. Add the peas and wine and cook until the wine evaporates. Season with thyme, salt and pepper to taste. Set aside.
4. Add the egg yolks and grated cheese to the cooked rice and mix well. Place the flour in a shallow bowl. Place the breadcrumbs in a separate shallow bowl. Set aside.
5. In a separate bowl, beat the egg whites briefly with a fork. Brush about ½ tsp of egg white on the palm of your hand, press 2 heaped tbsp rice into it and mould it into a hollow, cup-like shell. Fill the hollow with 1 tbsp of the meat mixture. Cover the filling with about 1 ½ tbsp of rice and use both hands to seal the filling inside and shape into a ball about the size of a small orange.

6. Roll each *arancina* (ball) first in flour, then in the remaining egg white and finally in the breadcrumbs.
7. Pour enough oil into a small saucepan to a depth of about 15cm. When it is very hot, deep-fry the rice balls two or three at a time, turning occasionally, until golden brown on all sides. Drain them on kitchen paper and serve warm.

✻ To check if the oil is sufficiently hot, drop a cube of bread in – it should brown immediately. If the oil isn't at the correct temperature for cooking the arancini, they will simply soak up the oil rather than crisp.

Marinated Peppers

Peperoni marinati

Serves 4

No antipasta platter is complete without this colourful peperonata, *in my opinion. The balsamic vinegar balances out the sweetness of the peppers. Pile this high on crusty bread for a delicious snack, then break off another chunk of bread for mopping up the sweet juices.*

100ml extra virgin olive oil
2 large onions, thinly sliced
1 green pepper, thinly sliced
2 yellow peppers, thinly sliced

1 red pepper, thinly sliced
1 sprig of rosemary
1 tbsp balsamic vinegar
salt and freshly ground black pepper

1. Heat the oil in a large, heavy-based frying pan. Add the onions, peppers and rosemary and sauté on a low heat for 10 minutes, until the vegetables are very tender. Remove from the heat and stir in the vinegar. Season to taste with salt and pepper. Serve hot or at room temperature.

✻ This will keep refrigerated for about 1 week, so make a double batch. It's also delicious added to a salad or sandwich.

Aubergine Parmigiana

Melanzane alla Parmigiana

Serves 6

Aside from pizza, this is probably the most famous dish to come out of Naples. Nowadays you'll find it all over Italy and beyond. I particularly enjoy a good parmigiana *not only as antipasta, but especially for lunch with a green salad and balsamic dressing.*

3 medium aubergines, sliced 2cm thick
salt and freshly ground black pepper
extra virgin olive oil
300ml tomato sauce (p. 130)

250g mozzarella, thinly sliced
1 bunch basil
100g freshly grated Parmesan

1. Preheat the oven to 180°C.
2. Place the aubergine slices in a colander, sprinkle with salt and allow them to degorge for about 30 minutes to let the bitter juices drain. Rinse and pat them dry.
3. Heat some oil in a frying pan and fry the aubergine in batches over a medium heat. Drain on kitchen paper and season to taste with salt and freshly ground black pepper.
4. Spread some tomato sauce over the bottom of a 25cm x 20cm baking dish. Cover with a layer of aubergine, followed by one-third of the mozzarella and a layer of basil leaves. Continue with another layer, ending with tomato sauce. Place the remaining mozzarella on top and finish with the grated Parmesan.
5. Bake for 20–25 minutes, until the cheese is golden around the edges.

* For a lighter version of this dish, grill or barbecue the aubergines rather than frying them and replace the mozzarella with ricotta.

Roasted Stuffed Peppers

Peperoni ripieni al forno

Serves 4 as a starter

I particularly like stuffed peppers as a starter, for lunch or simply for my vegetarian day. The sweetness of the roasted red peppers works well with the savoury filling. Sometimes I use feta instead of mozzarella – I admit it's not Italian, but it's delicious in the peppers.

2 red peppers
extra virgin olive oil
1 onion, finely chopped
2 garlic cloves, finely chopped
100g buffalo mozzarella, roughly chopped
150g breadcrumbs
3 anchovies, finely chopped (optional)

8 cherry tomatoes, diced
1 tsp chopped oregano
salt and freshly ground black pepper
10 black olives, sliced
2 tsp chopped flat-leaf parsley
green salad, to serve

1. Preheat the oven to 180°C.
2. Halve the peppers, including the stalks. Remove the membrane and seeds. Brush a baking tray with olive oil and place the peppers on it, cut side up.
3. Heat some olive oil in a frying pan. Cook the onion on a low heat for 7–10 minutes, until sweet in flavour. Add the garlic and cook for about 1 minute.
4. Transfer the onion and garlic to a bowl. Add the mozzarella, breadcrumbs, anchovies, cherry tomatoes and oregano. Season with salt and pepper to taste. Add a little oil and mix well.
5. Spoon the breadcrumb mixture into the peppers. Add the olives on top. Sprinkle with parsley and some olive oil.
6. Roast in the oven for about 40 minutes, until the peppers are fully cooked through. Serve with a green salad.

✳ *If you aren't partial to olives, replace them with some freshly grated Parmesan.*

Marinated Olives

Olive marinate

Purchasing marinated olives over the counter seems like such an easy option, but it's so much more fun (and tastier) to prepare them at home. Here are a few ideas for marinades. Allow at least 12 hours for the flavours to meld.

Black olives with preserved lemons, rosemary and extra virgin olive oil
Black olives with roasted peppers, capers, balsamic vinegar, basil and extra virgin olive oil
Green olives with parsley, chopped garlic, lemon juice and extra virgin olive oil
Green olives with orange zest, garlic, mint, chilli and extra virgin olive oil

✳ The leftover marinade can be used as a salad dressing.

Grilled Portobello Mushrooms with Lemon and Rosemary Oil

Funghi portobello alla griglia con limone e olio al rosmarino

Serves 4

I'm a big fan of mushrooms, so naturally I make this recipe quite a bit. I also add some extra ingredients to the breadcrumbs, depending on the mood and the contents of my fridge. For example, chopped red chilli or chopped hazelnuts mixed in with the crumbs work really well here.

for the grilled mushrooms:
4 medium portobello mushrooms, stems removed
extra virgin olive oil
salt and freshly ground black pepper
50g breadcrumbs
2 garlic cloves, diced
50g freshly grated Parmesan
zest of 1 lemon
2 tsp chopped parsley

for the lemon and rosemary oil:
zest and juice of 1 small lemon
salt and freshly ground black pepper
4 tbsp extra virgin olive oil
1 small sprig of rosemary, leaves chopped

green salad, to serve

1. Preheat the grill.
2. Brush the mushrooms on both sides with olive oil and season with salt and pepper.
3. Place the breadcrumbs, garlic, Parmesan, lemon zest and parsley in a bowl with a little seasoning. Add a little olive oil and spoon the mixture into the mushrooms.
4. Grill for 6–7 minutes, or until just cooked through.
5. Meanwhile, to make the lemon and rosemary oil, whisk the lemon zest and juice with a little salt and pepper. Gradually add the olive oil. Stir in the rosemary and check the seasoning.
6. Drizzle each mushroom with the lemon dressing and serve with a green salad on the side.

* Add chopped hazelnuts into the breadcrumb mix for an extra dimension to the recipe. If the mushrooms are particularly large, grill them first and then finish them in the oven preheated to 180°C for 10 minutes to ensure they're fully cooked through.

Chickpea Fritters

Panelle

Makes 30 fritters

Believed to be of Arab origin, these are a favourite snack in Sicily. This recipe is from Antonio and Bruna Fulvio from Palermo, and their hot tip on shaping the panelle *is to put the cooled dough into an empty Pringles carton, lightly oiled on the inside, and refrigerate. When ready to cook, push the dough out or cut the carton and slice as per the recipe.*

300g chickpea flour
900ml water
salt and freshly ground black pepper
2 tsp finely chopped oregano or rosemary
3 tbsp finely chopped parsley
olive oil or sunflower oil, for deep frying

1. Sieve the flour. Pour the water into a medium-large saucepan and whisk in the flour to ensure there are no lumps. Add salt and pepper to taste.
2. Cook over a medium heat for about 12–15 minutes, stirring constantly, until the mixture begins to pull away from the sides. Add the herbs. Check for seasoning again at this stage, as the mixture may need more salt and pepper. Leave to cool for 5 minutes.
3. Cut a 30cm length of baking parchment and spoon the mixture onto it. Spread the dough into a long strip and roll the paper over to form a sausage shape about 5cm in diameter. Refrigerate for 30 minutes.
4. When ready, remove the paper. With a very sharp knife, cut the dough into very thin slices (about ½cm).
5. Using a deep saucepan, pour in enough oil so that it's about 5cm deep. Heat the oil, and when it begins to shimmer, fry the *panelle* in batches, taking care not to overcrowd the pan, until golden brown, turning once. Drain on kitchen paper, sprinkle with salt and serve immediately.

✳ For a change of flavour, add some garlic and paprika.
    You could also add some lemon juice to the water, taking care that the total liquid is still 900ml.

Stuffed and Fried Courgette Blossoms

Fiori di zucca fritti e ripieni

Serves 4

Courgette blossoms are surprisingly tasty. I was very fortunate to have an unbelievable crop of these lovely golden orange blossoms in our cookery school garden this year. We had great fun coming up with ideas for stuffing – everything from precooked minced pork or chicken to mozzarella and anchovies (a Roman touch) went in. They are delicious and elegant.

250g ricotta
3 tbsp chopped mixed fresh herbs,
   e.g. chives, thyme, basil, parsley
1 garlic clove, minced
pinch of grated nutmeg

3 eggs
salt and freshly ground black pepper
12 courgette (zucchini) blossoms
250g flour
olive oil, for deep frying

1. For the filling, mix together the ricotta, fresh herbs, garlic, nutmeg and 1 egg in a bowl. Season with salt and pepper.
2. Remove the stamens from the courgette blossoms. Gently stuff each blossom with the mixture and twist the petals closed.
3. Heat the oil to 190°C in a deep fryer.
4. Whisk the remaining 2 eggs in a bowl. Divide the flour into two plates and season one plate of flour with salt and pepper.
5. First dip the blossoms into the flour without the seasoning, then into the egg and finally into the seasoned flour.
6. Fry the blossoms in batches, turning to lightly brown both sides. Drain on kitchen paper. Sprinkle with salt and serve immediately.

✱ It's also possible to shallow fry the courgette blossoms in a frying pan. Just turn them after 2-3 minutes to lightly colour both sides.

20

Crunchy Vegetables with Warm Anchovy Sauce

Bagna cauda

Serves 6 (E)

This is a famous sauce from the Piedmont region of Italy and it means 'hot bath'. I was given a fondue set years ago, and like most people, I never anticipated using it until I discovered this recipe. The sauce is served warm and vegetables are placed around it for dipping.

50g butter
4 garlic cloves, minced
10 anchovies canned in oil, minced
250ml extra virgin olive oil
zest of 1 lemon
salt and freshly ground black pepper
a selection of celery, radicchio and fennel, washed and trimmed into pieces
crusty bread, cut into 3cm cubes

1. Melt the butter in a saucepan over a low heat and add the garlic. Cook for 1 minute, until softened. Add the anchovies and slowly pour in the olive oil, followed by the lemon zest. Cook over a low heat, stirring from time to time. Season with salt and pepper. Keep warm.
2. Arrange the vegetables around a platter. Place the sauce into a warm bowl in the centre and arrange the bread on the side.

＊ I really like dipping artichoke leaves into bagna cauda. To prepare the artichoke, cut off the thorns and leaves of the stalk. Pull off and discard the tougher outer leaves. Trim the stalk, then peel with a vegetable peeler. Prise open the centre of the choke. The centre will be furry, almost thistle like. Cut this out and discard it. Place in a bowl of lemon juice with water to prevent them from discolouring, then steam until softened.

Tuscan Bread Salad

Panzanella

Serves 4–6

This is a popular dish anywhere from Rome northwards to Tuscany. The idea is that it uses up all the summer vegetables and leftover bread, so the bread must be stale for this to work. I enjoy this salad with grilled chicken or fish or as part of a buffet for BBQs. It's important that it isn't mixed too far in advance, as the bread will go soggy. And while it might seem like there is a lot of slicing, dicing and chopping to do, the results are truly worth it.

for the red wine vinaigrette:

4 tbsp red wine vinegar
½ tsp Dijon mustard
1 shallot, minced
130ml extra virgin olive oil
salt and freshly ground black pepper
1 tsp sugar
1 tbsp minced fresh herbs, such as chives and parsley (optional)

for the Tuscan bread salad:

150g stale or toasted Italian bread, cubed
5 anchovy fillets, sliced (optional, or to taste)
4 large tomatoes, diced
2 garlic cloves, minced
2 celery stalks, sliced thinly on the diagonal
1 red pepper, diced
1 yellow pepper, diced
½ cucumber, deseeded and diced
1 tsp capers, chopped
1 sprig of basil, chopped

1. To make the vinaigrette, combine the vinegar, mustard and shallot and leave for 20–30 minutes for the flavours to meld. Slowly whisk in the olive oil so that the mixture emulsifies. Adjust the seasoning with salt, pepper and sugar. Add the herbs, if desired.
2. To prepare the salad, combine everything in a large bowl. Add the vinaigrette and toss to coat. Serve immediately.

✳ Sometimes I replace the anchovies with a tin of drained tuna. It's not Italian, but it's delicious!

Courgette and Thyme Frittata

Frittata di zucchine e timo

Serves 6

I often make this lovely Italian omelette for lunch or a TV dinner. It is full of goodness, very filling and delicious with a crisp garden salad.

4 tbsp extra virgin olive oil, divided
1 onion, finely sliced
1 tsp chopped thyme
2 medium courgettes, cut into 1 ½cm dice
7 eggs, free-range and organic if possible
1 tsp chopped parsley
50g freshly grated Parmesan
salt and freshly ground black pepper

1. Heat 2 tbsp olive oil in an ovenproof frying pan. Add the onions and thyme and sauté on a low heat for 7–10 minutes, until the onions are soft and slightly caramelised. Add the diced courgettes and cook over a medium heat for 5 minutes. Using a slotted spoon, lift the onions and courgettes from the pan and discard the remaining oil.
2. In a bowl, mix together the eggs, parsley, Parmesan, salt and pepper. Gently stir in the onions and courgettes until they are all coated with the egg mixture.
3. Wipe out the pan with kitchen paper and heat the remaining 2 tbsp oil. Add the egg and courgette mixture to the pan and cook over a very low heat, until the egg begins to set. To prevent the frittata from sticking, use a metal spatula to lift it and allow the uncooked egg to run underneath.
4. Preheat the grill to a medium heat. Once the frittata has set around the edges but is still unset in the middle, transfer under the grill for about 5 minutes, until the centre is set and golden.
5. To remove it from the pan, place a plate over the frying pan and invert the pan. The frittata should just pop onto the plate (take care, as the pan will be very hot). Cut into wedges and serve garnished with parsley.

✳ For a crispy, cheesy topping, sprinkle some grated mozzarella on top just as the grilling is almost finished.

Caprese Salad

Insalata Caprese

Serves 4

The choice of tomatoes is crucial to this recipe. It will only be a success with fresh, ripe, red tomatoes. I get Brandywine tomatoes from An Tairseach, our local organic farm. These are huge, sweet, juicy tomatoes and Insalata Caprese *is the first recipe I plan as I head home with my precious stash.*

650g ripe tomatoes
250g mozzarella cheese
3 tbsp chopped or shredded fresh basil leaves
150g green olives
60ml extra virgin olive oil
sea salt and freshly ground black pepper

1. Slice the tomatoes and the mozzarella cheese about ½cm thick.
2. Alternate the mozzarella and tomato slices on a presentation platter, overlapping them. Sprinkle with the olives, basil, olive oil, sea salt and pepper.

✳ As with the tomatoes, the quality of the olive oil is crucial. If you aren't satisfied with your olive oil, consider making a balsamic dressing with some garlic, balsamic vinegar, extra virgin olive oil, salt and pepper.

✳ If the tomatoes aren't sufficiently sweet, halve them and remove the seeds. Place them on an oiled baking tray and sprinkle with a little sugar, salt and thyme. Roast in an oven preheated to 180°C for 20-30 minutes. Serve cooled with the mozzarella in the salad.

Seared Scallops with Fennel Salad and Orange Basil Dressing

Cappesante ai ferri con insalata di finocchi e salsa all'arancia e basilica

Serves 6

Claudio needs a regular drip feed of his own cuisine! He hails from Palermo, located in the Conca d'Oro – the Valley of Gold, so called because of the abundance of wonderful golden orange groves on the plains of this city. It's a spectacular sight in the early spring.

I had this dish in a restaurant in Syracuse and I thought I had died and gone to fennel heaven! Scallops are wonderful in March, so I recommend this recipe for spring entertaining.

for the scallops and fennel salad:
2 medium fennel bulbs, thinly sliced
1 medium head of radicchio, quartered
   and thinly sliced
4 oranges, skinned and sliced ½cm thick
18 large scallops
salt and freshly ground black pepper
2 tbsp butter, divided
juice of 1 lemon

for the orange basil dressing:
250ml olive oil
zest and juice of 1 orange
1 tbsp chopped basil
25ml white wine vinegar
1 tsp Dijon mustard
1 tbsp honey (or more to taste)
salt and freshly ground black pepper

1. To make the dressing, purée all the dressing ingredients in a food processor (or whisk by hand, but chop the basil very finely in this case). Season to taste and add more honey as required (some oranges are sweeter than others, so the amount of honey will depend on this).
2. Combine the fennel, radicchio and orange slices in a large bowl. Add about 175ml of the vinaigrette and toss to combine. Set aside.
3. Separate the corals from the main body of the scallops. Pat dry and season them all with salt and pepper. Melt 1 tbsp butter in a large, heavy-based non-stick frying pan over a high heat. Add the scallops and sauté until golden on both sides and just opaque in the middle. This should take about 4–5 minutes in total. Transfer to a warm plate and cover with foil to keep them warm.

4. Put the remaining butter in the pan and add the corals, which will cook faster (about 2 minutes). When ready to serve, add the corals to the plate with the scallops and squeeze over some fresh lemon juice.

5. Divide the salad among 6 plates. Place 3 scallops on top of the salad on each plate, with the corals beside them. Drizzle with the remaining vinaigrette and serve.

✳ Chop the basil last, just before you add it to the dressing, otherwise it will turn black. Similarly, it's best to make this dressing as you need it, as the basil won't retain its lovely bright green shade.

Crostini, Bruschetta and Fettunta

Both crostini and bruschetta are slices of bread with toppings, but there is a difference. Bruschetta tends to be slices of ciabatta about 2cm thick, grilled and then rubbed with garlic. Traditionally, bruschetta was prepared with a fresh tomato topping, but nowadays anything goes. Fettunta is a Tuscan bruschetta. The bread for crostini is smaller, often a French loaf, usually one or two bites in size and only about 1cm thick. It's also toasted and topped with an array of delicious flavours.

Crostini

As a TV snack or with drinks when friends come round, crostini ticks all the boxes for food heaven. There are hundreds of options for toppings, so there's always something to suit everyone. Here are a few of my favourites.

How to prepare the base
1. Preheat the grill.
2. Use thin slices of country-style white bread (crusts trimmed, if you like). Brush both sides of the bread slices with a little extra virgin olive oil and place on a baking sheet.
3. Toast the bread slices for 2–3 minutes per side, until golden – keep watching! Cool completely before using. Top with any of the following.

Tomato and Caper Crostini

Crostini ai pomodori e capperi

Makes 18 crostini

1 ½ tbsp capers, roughly chopped
1 tsp extra virgin olive oil
freshly ground black pepper

10 cherry tomatoes, sliced
basil leaves
Parmesan shavings, to finish

1. Combine the capers with the olive oil and add pepper to taste. Add in the sliced tomatoes and gently mix.
2. Place 1 or 2 basil leaves onto the crostini, then place slices of the cherry tomato mixture on top.
3. Just before serving, finish with Parmesan shavings and a drizzle of extra virgin olive oil. Serve immediately.

* If capers aren't to your liking, try black olives as an alternative.

Goat's Cheese and Chive Crostini

Crostini ai formaggio di capra e erba

Makes about 15–18 crostini

200g soft goat's cheese
2 tbsp chopped chives, plus extra to garnish

2 tbsp extra virgin olive oil
salt and freshly ground black pepper

1. Gently mash the goat's cheese, chives and olive oil together. Season with salt and pepper and spoon onto the crostini. Garnish with chives. This pâté can be kept for up to 2 days in the fridge.

* This pâté works well not only on crostini, but as a dip on a platter with carrot and celery sticks, breadsticks (p. 51), carrot and parsnip crisps or mini sweet corn.

Goat's cheese and chive crostini (left), tomato and caper crostini (centre) and chicken liver crostini (right)

Chicken Liver Crostini

Crostini al fegato di pollo

Makes 18–20 crostini

300g chicken livers, trimmed and cleaned
extra virgin olive oil
1 onion, finely chopped
75g pancetta or smoked bacon, cut into 2cm dice
1 garlic clove, finely chopped

1 tsp chopped thyme
salt and freshly ground black pepper
4 tbsp Marsala
200g butter, softened

1. Rinse the livers in cold water and pat them dry.
2. Heat some olive oil in a pan. Sauté the onion on a low heat for 7–10 minutes, until soft. Add the pancetta (or bacon) and cook for 3–4 minutes on a high heat. Add the chicken livers, garlic, thyme and seasoning and sauté for 4–5 minutes, until the livers are fully cooked. Stir in the Marsala and sauté for a further 1 minute.
3. Place in a food processor together with the softened butter and blend until smooth.

＊ This is best made 24 hours before using. If you want a very smooth pâté, pass it through a fine sieve.

＊ You could use brandy instead of Marsala.

33

Bruschetta

When my friends come around I usually make a selection of *bruschette*, arrange them on platters and guests dig in. It's a lovely, informal way of entertaining and often breaks the ice.

Prosciutto, Pesto, Walnut and Fig Bruschetta

Bruschetta con prosciutto, pesto, noci e fichi

Makes 12 **E**

12 ciabatta slices, brushed with extra virgin olive oil and toasted on both sides
1 garlic clove, halved
50ml walnut pesto (p. 136)
12 slices prosciutto
6 ripe figs, each cut into 6 wedges
15 walnut halves, roughly chopped and toasted
extra virgin olive oil

1. Rub the toasted ciabatta with the cut side of the garlic cloves and follow with a generous layer of the pesto. Place a slice of prosciutto on top, followed by 3 fig wedges. Scatter over the walnuts and glaze with a drizzle of olive oil.

✳ For vegetarians, use a soft goat's cheese instead of the prosciutto.

Prosciutto, pesto, walnut and fig bruschetta (top), tomato fettunta (middle) and mushroom, Parmesan and truffle oil bruschetta (bottom)

Mushroom, Parmesan and Truffle Oil Bruschetta

Bruschetta ai funghi, Parmigiano e olio al tartufo

Makes 12 **E**

12 ciabatta slices, brushed with olive oil and toasted on both sides
1 garlic clove, halved
250g wild mushrooms or your favourite selection
1 tbsp truffle-infused extra virgin olive oil
1 tbsp butter
2 shallots, finely chopped
2 tbsp Marsala
salt and freshly ground black pepper
2 tbsp chopped parsley
Parmesan shavings, to finish

1. Rub the toasted ciabatta with the cut side of the garlic.
2. Wipe the mushrooms clean and slice them.
3. Heat the oil and butter in a frying pan. Add the shallots and sauté until lightly golden. Add the mushrooms and cook for about 2–3 minutes. Add the Marsala and simmer until the alcohol has evaporated, about 2 minutes. Season with salt and pepper and add the parsley.
4. To assemble, spoon some of the mushroom mixture onto the bread. Place a few Parmesan shavings on top. Drizzle with a little more truffle-infused olive oil and serve.

* Truffle oil is one of life's little luxuries. I have often made this recipe with alternative flavoured oils, such as lemon or rosemary oil.

Tomato Fettunta

Fettunta al pomodoro

Makes 12

Fettunta is Tuscan bruschetta. It was originally associated with the month of November, as the locals celebrated the harvest of the olives and the new olive oil of the season. Bread is toasted, garlic rubbed over and then the finest extra virgin olive oil you can get, first press, is generously drizzled over. Nowadays it's available all year round and sometimes served with tomatoes.

12 ciabatta slices, brushed with extra virgin olive oil and toasted on both sides
1 garlic clove, halved
extra virgin olive oil, preferably first press
salt and freshly ground black pepper
6 ripe tomatoes, deseeded and chopped
100g sun-dried tomatoes, chopped
1 red onion, finely sliced
a generous handful of basil leaves

1. Rub the toasted ciabatta with the cut side of the garlic. Drizzle with a little olive oil and season with salt and pepper.
2. Mix the chopped tomatoes, sun-dried tomatoes and red onion together in a bowl. Spoon the mixture onto the ciabatta. Tear the basil leaves and scatter them over the *fettunta*. Drizzle with more olive oil and serve immediately.

* This recipe only works if the tomatoes are absolutely ripe, red and sweet. Try cherry tomatoes on the vine, halved, as an alternative.

Bread, Pizzas and Calzones

Rosemary Focaccia
Focaccia al rosmarino

Tomato Focaccia
Focaccia ai pomodori

Mozzarella and Pancetta
Filled Bread
Stromboli

Breadsticks
Grissini

Italian Flat Bread
Piadina

Sicilian Pizza Bread
Sfincione

Basic Pizza Dough

Pizza Toppings

Margherita

Marinara

Artichoke and Pancetta
Carciofi e pancetta

Roasted Summer Vegetables
Verdure al forno

Leek, Gorgonzola and Walnut
Porri, Gorgonzola e noci

Parma Ham, Chicory and Olive
Prosciutto, endivia e olive

Pancetta, Spinach and Three
Cheese Calzone
*Calzone ai tre formaggi,
pancetta e spinaci*

Rosemary Focaccia

Focaccia al rosmarino

Makes 2 loaves

The aroma of the rosemary toasting as the bread cooks will draw neighbours from near and far. As yeast breads go, focaccia is very easy to make. Like all yeast breads, patience is a key ingredient. I leave my dough to rise in a hot press or even outside on a sunny day, and I know a lady in Sicily who leaves the dough on the bonnet of her car after driving on a cooler day.

2 ½ tsp dried yeast (or 1 x 7g sachet)
1 tbsp sugar
450ml lukewarm water (more if required)
700g Italian '00' or strong white flour
2 tsp salt
1 tbsp extra virgin olive oil
2 large sprigs of rosemary
sea salt

1. Mix the yeast and sugar in the lukewarm water and allow the yeast to activate. When the yeast is frothy, it's ready to use.
2. Sieve the flour into a mixing bowl and add the salt, olive oil and yeast mixture. Mix to a soft dough, adding more flour or water as required. Knead until the dough is very pliable, which should take about 7–10 minutes by hand.
3. Leave the dough to rise in a well-oiled bowl covered with cling film until the dough has trebled in size and is springy to the touch, which will take 2–3 hours. This will rise best in a warm, draught-free place, e.g. a hot press or near a cooker or oven.
4. When it has risen, knock it back and place onto a lightly floured surface. Knead it again by hand for 2–3 minutes.
5. Divide the dough into 2 pieces and roll or press them out until the dough is 1cm thick. Place the dough onto 2 oiled baking sheets. Flatten the dough and push it into the corners of the sheet, then make indentations on the top of the dough with your fingertips. Drizzle the surface with olive oil, pull the leaves from the rosemary stalk and scatter them, along with the sea salt, on top of the dough. Allow the dough to rise again for 30–45 minutes in a warm place.

6. Meanwhile, preheat the oven to 230°C. Bake for 5 minutes, then reduce the temperature to 200°C and bake for a further 10 minutes. Remove from the oven and allow to cool, then loosen from the pan and cut into squares.

✳ A stand mixer is very useful for bread making. Use the dough hook to knead for 5-7 minutes, then continue with the recipe by placing the dough in a well-oiled bowl for rising.

✳ Replace the rosemary with chopped sage or oregano and tuck some small balls of mozzarella into the indentations for a delicious bread.

Tomato Focaccia

Focaccia ai pomodori

Makes 1 tray

Contrary to the fun jibes I get in my cookery school, the potatoes in this recipe is not my way of bringing a bit of Irishness into a traditional Italian recipe. This is a lovely recipe and the dough is surprisingly light.

2 ½ tsp dried yeast (or 1 x 7g sachet)	2 tsp salt
1 tbsp sugar	1 tbsp extra virgin olive oil
425ml lukewarm water (more if required)	20 cherry tomatoes
200g freshly mashed potato	2 tsp chopped marjoram (or 1 tsp dried oregano)
600g Italian '00' or strong white flour	sea salt

1. Mix the yeast and sugar in the lukewarm water and allow the yeast to activate. When the yeast is frothy, it's ready to use. Add the mashed potato to the yeast and stir.
2. Sieve the flour into a mixing bowl and add the salt, olive oil and yeast/potato mixture. Mix to a loose dough, adding more flour or water as required. Knead until the dough is very pliable, which should take about 7–10 minutes by hand. The dough may be a little sticky.
3. Leave the dough to rise in a well-oiled bowl covered with cling film until the dough has trebled in size and is springy to the touch, which will take 2–3 hours. This will rise best in a warm, draught-free place, e.g. a hot press or near a cooker or oven.
4. When it has risen, knock it back, gently knead it again on a lightly floured surface and place onto an oiled baking tray. Flatten the dough and push it into the corners of the tin. Brush with oil, cover with cling film and leave to rise in a warm place until it doubles in size, which will take about 45 minutes.
5. Preheat the oven to 200°C.
6. Dimple the dough using your fingertips, then place the tomatoes in the dimples. Sprinkle with the marjoram or oregano and some sea salt and drizzle with a little olive oil. Bake for about 45 minutes. Allow to cool, then loosen from the pan and cut into squares.

* To vary this recipe, add olives, pancetta and/or sun-dried tomatoes. Not only are they delicious toppings for focaccia, but they're usually sitting in our fridges waiting to be used!

Mozarella and Pancetta Filled Bread

Stromboli

Serves 6–8

Of all the breads I make, this is my favourite. The inhabitants of the volcanic island Stromboli, off the coast of Sicily, developed this bread. The dough is rolled with all sorts of wonderful ingredients, such as olives, sun-dried tomatoes, mozzarella and pancetta. When you bite into the bread, the experience is a volcanic explosion of flavours and colours that light up the taste buds.

1 rounded tsp dried yeast (or ½ x 7g sachet)
½ tsp sugar
225ml lukewarm water (more if required)
350g Italian '00' or strong white flour
½ tsp salt
2 tsp extra virgin olive oil, plus extra for drizzling

150ml tomato sauce (p. 130)
150g grated mozzarella
100g pancetta, roughly chopped
3 tbsp sliced black olives
3 medium thyme sprigs
½ tsp coarse sea salt

1. Mix the yeast and sugar in the lukewarm water and allow the yeast to activate. When the yeast is frothy, it's ready to use.
2. Sieve the flour into a mixing bowl and add the salt, olive oil and yeast mixture. Mix to a soft, loose dough, adding more flour or water as required. Knead until the dough is very pliable, which should take about 7–10 minutes by hand.
3. Leave the dough to rise in a well-oiled bowl covered with cling film until the dough has trebled in size and is springy to the touch, which will take 2–3 hours. This will rise best in a warm, draught-free place, e.g. a hot press or near a cooker or oven.
4. When it has risen, knock it back and place onto a lightly floured surface. Knead it again by hand for 2–3 minutes.
5. Roll out the dough to a 33cm x 28cm rectangle about 5mm–1cm thick.
6. Spread the dough with tomato sauce and sprinkle over the mozzarella, pancetta, olives and a little of the thyme.

7. Roll up like a Swiss roll, tucking in the ends. Transfer to a lightly oiled baking sheet with the join underneath. Cover with a damp cloth and leave for 30–45 minutes in a warm, draught-free place.
8. Preheat the oven to 200°C.
9. Remove the cloth and pierce the roll with a large fork about 5 times, through to the baking sheet. Lightly brush the surface with olive oil and sprinkle over the sea salt. Tuck the remaining thyme sprigs into the surface of the dough.
10. Bake for 30–35 minutes, until cooked through and pale golden. Drizzle over a little extra virgin olive oil and transfer to a wire rack to cool.

✳ While moving well away from the original recipe, I vary this dish depending on the mood. I fill the stromboli with anything from ricotta, spinach and nutmeg to soft goat's cheese and red pepper pesto.

Breadsticks

Grissini

Makes 22–25 breadsticks

Why buy breadsticks when they're such fun to make? My children especially love trying this recipe. I usually make a selection with a variety of toppings, not only for flavour but for colour too.

1 rounded tsp dried yeast (or ½ x 7g sachet)
½ tsp sugar
250ml lukewarm water
325g Italian '00' or strong white flour
1 tsp salt
1 egg + 1 tbsp milk or water, beaten

Topping options: coarse salt, cumin seeds, poppy and sesame seeds, coarsely ground black pepper or fresh chopped rosemary

1. Mix the yeast and sugar in the lukewarm water and allow the yeast to activate. When the yeast is frothy, it's ready to use. Stir in the flour and salt to make a medium-soft dough.
2. Knead the dough on a lightly floured surface until it's elastic and satiny, which should take about 8–10 minutes. Add only the minimum amount of additional flour needed to keep the dough from sticking.
3. Put the dough in a large mixing bowl, cover it with cling film and let it rise in a warm, draught-free place until it has doubled in size, which should take about 1 ½ hours.
4. Preheat the oven to 220°C.
5. Punch down the dough and turn it out onto a lightly floured surface. Roll it into a rectangle about 22cm long and 1cm thick.
6. Cut the dough into 1cm strips. Brush one side of the strip with the egg wash, then dip in a topping. Put one hand at each end of the strip and simultaneously turn one hand forward and the other backwards to twist the strip, then place on a lightly oiled baking sheet. Repeat this process with the other strips.
7. Bake for 8–12 minutes, depending on size, until golden brown and crisp. Cool on a wire rack.

✳ Breadsticks are usually baked without a final rising, but for a lighter result, let the shaped dough rise for about 10 minutes before baking.

Italian Flat Bread

Piadina

Serves 6

Piadina is a thin, flat bread that's fairly chewy and soft. The farmwomen in Romagna cooked it on a terracotta dish called a testo *over hot coals. Nowadays they're street food. Traditionally they were made with lard rather than olive oil, which reminds me of a Mexican tortilla. They're usually filled with cheeses, salami or ham, roasted vegetables and sometimes even with sweet fillings.*

400g Italian '00' or strong white flour
60ml extra virgin olive oil
70ml milk
½ tsp salt
approx. 100ml warm water

Serving suggestions: Fill with your favourite ingredients, such as roasted peppers, basil pesto and rocket or sliced ripe plum tomatoes, fresh mozzarella and basil with a drizzle of olive oil.

1. Place the flour in a mixing bowl and make a hollow in the middle. Pour in the oil, milk and salt. Add enough warm water to make a soft dough.
2. Place the dough on a floured surface and knead for about 5–6 minutes, until smooth.
3. Cut the dough into pieces about the size of a medium scone. Roll each piece out into a very thin disc.
4. Heat a heavy-based frying pan or griddle pan with a little oil. Cook the dough over a medium heat for about 12 seconds on each side. Turn over, prick with a fork and continue to cook for a further 2–3 minutes. Remove from the heat and add your chosen fillings.

* I add finely chopped black olives and thyme to the dough for extra flavour.

Sicilian Pizza Bread

Sfincione

Makes 1 tray

I am most grateful to our local baker in Ballestrate, Solina Testagrossa, who taught me this recipe. It's unusual for professional bakers to share their secrets, so I know how fortunate I am having Solina as a friend. The day she taught me, I slowed down the process through my many questions, which resulted in the sfincione *arriving an hour late from the ovens. It nearly caused a riot in the bakery, such was the queue of* sfincione *fans. I've adjusted this recipe a little to reflect ingredients that are more readily available, such as using mozzarella instead of caciocavallo cheese.*

for the base:
270ml warm water
3 tsp sugar
1 tsp dried yeast
250g Italian '00' or strong white flour
100g semolina flour (*grano duro*)
1 tsp salt
50ml extra virgin olive oil

for the topping:
extra virgin olive oil
1 large onion, diced
4 anchovies, minced
175g buffalo mozzarella, sliced
450ml passata or tomato sauce (p. 130)
75g breadcrumbs, toasted
75g grated Pecorino (or Parmesan)
1 tbsp dried oregano

1. Pour the water into a large jug, add the sugar and stir to dissolve. Sprinkle the yeast over the water and let it sit for several minutes to dissolve. When the yeast is frothy, it's ready to use.
2. Mix the flours and salt in a bowl. Make a well in the centre and pour in the yeast mixture.
3. Knead the dough on a lightly floured surface until it's elastic and satiny, which should take about 8–10 minutes, adding only the minimum amount of additional flour needed to keep the dough from sticking. Finally, knead in the olive oil (it might be cleaner to do this in a mixing bowl).
4. Put the dough in a large well-oiled mixing bowl, cover it with cling film or a damp tea towel and let it rise in a warm, draught-free place until doubled in size, which should take about 2 hours.
5. Meanwhile, heat a little olive oil in a frying pan. Sauté the diced onion on a low heat for 7–10 minutes, until softened. Set aside.

6. Preheat the oven to 180°C.
7. When the dough is ready, punch the air out and knead it on a lightly floured surface for 2 minutes. Flour the baking tray and place the dough on the tray, pressing it down to fill the tray completely.
8. Arrange the onion and anchovies on top, followed by the sliced cheese and lastly the tomato sauce. Mix the breadcrumbs with the grated Pecorino and oregano, then sprinkle them in an even layer over the sauce.
9. Bake the *sfincione* for about 25 minutes, until it sounds hollow when you tap the bottom.

✳ Another Solina trick is to cut this with a scissors, as it makes a nice clean cut without displacing the topping.

Basic Pizza Dough

Makes one 30cm x 40cm rectangle or three 30cm rounds

Pizza parties are very popular at my home. I simply make the bases and let everyone add their own toppings. We even finish with sweet pizzas for dessert – mascarpone, strawberries and mango with a crumble topping. The Roman pizzas are my favourite. These super-thin treats are topped with anything that's in season, including courgette flowers, and finished with mozarella from Campania. Yum!

1 rounded tsp dried yeast (or ½ x 7g sachet)
½ tsp sugar
150ml lukewarm water (more if required)
250g Italian '00' or strong white flour
1 tsp extra virgin olive oil
½ tsp salt

1. Mix the yeast and sugar in the lukewarm water and allow the yeast to activate. When the yeast is frothy, it's ready to use.
2. Sieve the flour into a mixing bowl and add the salt, olive oil and yeast mixture. Mix to a loose dough, adding more flour or water as required. Knead until the dough is very pliable, which should take about 5 minutes using the dough hook of a stand mixer or 5–10 minutes by hand.
3. Leave the dough to rise in a well-oiled bowl covered with cling film until the dough has trebled in size and is springy to the touch, which will take about 2 hours. This will rise best in a warm, draught-free place, e.g. a hot press or near a cooker or oven.
4. Preheat the oven to 230°C.
5. When it has risen, knock it back and place onto a lightly floured surface. Knead it again by hand for 2–3 minutes.
6. Roll out or stretch the dough with your hands onto a lightly oiled pizza pan/screen or baking sheet. Finish with toppings and bake as per the recipes on pp. 56–64.

＊ While not authentic, I've found that if I refrigerate the dough after knocking it back for about 1½ hours, it rolls out into a lovely thin base and doesn't spring back as much, thus resulting in a thin, crispy pizza.

* To avoid a soggy centre, brush the dough lightly with olive oil, leaving a 1cm rim around the edge. This forms a barrier to prevent the sauce from seeping into the dough.

* Sprinkle some semolina on the baking sheet so that the bases don't stick.

* Add 1 tsp chopped herbs and 1 tbsp chopped sun-dried tomatoes to the pizza dough for an interesting variation (add to the flour before adding the liquid).

Pizza Toppings

✳ ✳ ✳ ✳ ✳

Margherita

Makes enough topping for 1 rectangle or 3 rounds

As this classic originated in Naples, it's also known as the pizza napoletana.

extra virgin olive oil
250ml tomato sauce (p. 130)
salt and freshly ground black pepper
200g mozzarella, sliced
1 ½ tbsp freshly grated Parmesan (optional)
12 basil leaves, shredded

1. Preheat the oven to 230°C.
2. Brush the pizza base lightly with olive oil, leaving a 1cm rim around the edge.
3. Spread the tomato sauce evenly over the top, then drizzle with olive oil. Season with salt and pepper. Top with the mozzarella and bake for about 10–12 minutes.
4. To serve, drizzle with a little more olive oil and sprinkle with Parmesan and shredded basil leaves.

Marinara

Makes enough topping for 1 rectangle or 3 rounds

Marinara means 'sailor style'. No cheese is used, as it would not always have been available on the boats. It's definitely a topping for garlic lovers. Use very ripe tomatoes and fresh garlic for that intense, sweet, fruity flavour.

extra virgin olive oil
350ml tomato sauce (p. 130)
salt and freshly ground black pepper

5 garlic cloves, finely sliced
2 tsp chopped parsley

1. Preheat the oven to 230°C.
2. Brush the pizza base lightly with olive oil, leaving a 1cm rim around the edge.
3. Spread the tomato sauce evenly over the base and season with salt and pepper to taste. Add the sliced garlic and drizzle with more olive oil.
4. Bake for about 10–12 minutes. Drizzle with a little oil and sprinkle over the parsley.

Artichoke and Pancetta

Carciofi e pancetta

Makes enough topping for 1 rectangle or 3 rounds

extra virgin olive oil
150ml tomato sauce (p. 130)
1 x 250g jar of artichokes, drained and sliced
9 slices pancetta, cut into small pieces

12 pitted black olives, halved
1 small bunch of thyme, finely chopped
zest of 1 lemon

1. Preheat the oven to 230°C.
2. Brush the pizza base lightly with olive oil, leaving a 1cm rim around the edge.
3. Spread the tomato sauce evenly over the base, followed by the artichokes. Layer with pancetta, followed by olives and thyme. Lastly, sprinkle with the lemon zest.
4. Bake for 10–12 minutes and serve immediately.

Roasted Summer Vegetables

Verdure al forno

Makes enough topping for 1 rectangle or 3 rounds

1 yellow pepper, deseeded and cut into strips
1 red pepper, deseeded and cut into strips
1 medium aubergine, sliced
3 garlic cloves
1 courgette, sliced diagonally
2 red onions, sliced into wedges
extra virgin olive oil
2 sprigs of rosemary
200ml tomato sauce (p. 130)
freshly grated Parmesan
salt and freshly ground black pepper

1. Preheat the oven to 220°C.
2. Place all the vegetables into a roasting tin, drizzle with olive oil and add the rosemary sprigs. Roast for 30–35 minutes, until the vegetables are tender.
3. Brush the pizza base lightly with olive oil, leaving a 1cm rim around the edge.
4. Spread the tomato sauce evenly over the base, then arrange the vegetables on top. Sprinkle with Parmesan and season with salt and pepper.
5. Bake for about 10–12 minutes. Drizzle with a little oil and serve immediately.

✳ Use thyme instead of rosemary and add a squeeze of lemon juice to the roasted vegetables.

Leek, Gorgonzola and Walnut

Porri, Gorgonzola e noci

Makes enough topping for 1 rectangle or 3 rounds

extra virgin olive oil
3 leeks, sliced
salt and freshly ground black pepper
200g Gorgonzola cheese, crumbed
100g walnuts, roughly chopped

1. Heat some olive oil in a saucepan. Add the sliced leeks and allow to lightly cook over a low heat for about 10 minutes, until soft. Leave to cool.
2. Preheat the oven to 220°C.
3. Brush the pizza base lightly with olive oil, leaving a 1cm rim around the edge. Parbake the base for 6 minutes. Remove from the oven, then turn it down to 190°C.
4. Spread the leeks over the base and season with salt and pepper. Crumble over the Gorgonzola and then sprinkle with the walnuts.
5. Bake for a further 5 minutes, then serve immediately.

Parma Ham, Chicory and Olive

Prosciutto, endivia e olive

Makes enough topping for 1 rectangle or 3 rounds

extra virgin olive oil
150ml tomato sauce (p. 130)
12 slices buffalo mozzarella
4 tbsp chopped parsley, divided
1 head of chicory (Belgian endive), thinly sliced lengthways
4 slices Parma ham
freshly ground black pepper
16 black olives, pitted and halved
2 tbsp freshly grated Parmesan

1. Preheat the oven to 220°C.
2. Brush the pizza base lightly with olive oil, leaving a 1cm rim around the edge.
3. Spread the tomato sauce evenly over the base and drizzle with a little olive oil. Add the mozzarella slices and half the parsley. Arrange the chicory on top, followed by the Parma ham. Season with pepper and scatter with olives.
4. Bake for 15 minutes. Sprinkle with the Parmesan and remaining parsley and serve immediately.

*Leek, Gorgonzola and walnut pizza (left),
Parma ham, chicory and olive pizza (top right)
and artichoke and pancetta pizza (bottom left)*

Pancetta, Spinach and Three Cheese Calzone

Calzone ai tre formaggi, pancetta e spinaci

Makes 1 large calzone

This is an unusual calzone and is serious comfort food. Do take care with adding salt, as there is already salt in the pancetta, the Parmesan and the tomato sauce.

1 x basic pizza dough (p. 55)
extra virgin olive oil
200g fresh spinach, cooked and squeezed to remove excess liquid
100g grated mozzarella
100g pancetta lardons, fried in a little olive oil
100ml tomato sauce (p. 130)
pinch of hot chilli flakes, to taste
3 tbsp freshly grated Parmesan
75g ricotta cheese
pinch of nutmeg
salt and freshly ground black pepper

1. Preheat the oven to 200°C.
2. Stretch the dough into a 20cm circle and brush lightly with olive oil, leaving a 1cm rim around the edge.
3. Place the cooked spinach over one half of the circle, making sure to leave a clean 1cm rim around the edge. Layer each ingredient on top of another, beginning with mozzarella, then top with pancetta, tomato sauce, chilli flakes, Parmesan, ricotta cheese, nutmeg and salt and pepper.
4. Fold the empty half of dough over the ingredients and press the outer edges together with your fingers, ensuring they are fully closed.
5. Bake for 15–20 minutes. Check after 10 minutes and cover with foil if it's browning too quickly.
6. When cooked, remove from the oven, brush with a little olive oil and serve immediately.

✳ If you're having trouble sealing the calzone, brush the edges very lightly with a little beaten egg and then seal.

Soups

Leek and Lentil Soup with Parmesan Toasts
Zuppa di porro e lenticchie con crostini di Parmigiano

Tuscan Bean Soup with Toasted Garlic
Pasta e fagioli

Tomato Soup
Zuppa di pomodoro

Mussel Soup
Zuppa di cozze

Leek and Lentil Soup with Parmesan Toasts

Zuppa di porro e lenticchie con crostini di Parmigiano

Serves 6–8

A simple peasant dish, this is best made the day before and reheated. My husband grew up on Sicilian lentils, so this is by far his favourite soup. I like to serve Parmesan toasts with this soup, not only for flavour but also for colour.

for the leek and lentil soup:
extra virgin olive oil, for frying
3 leeks, finely sliced
200g pancetta, diced
3 garlic cloves, diced
2 celery stalks, finely diced
2 carrots, finely diced
2 sprigs of thyme
150ml white wine
225g dried Puy lentils
1 ¾ litres vegetable stock
salt and freshly ground black pepper
2 tbsp freshly grated Parmesan

for the Parmesan toasts:
6 x 1 ½ cm slices of ciabatta
extra virgin olive oil
1 garlic clove, halved
2 tbsp freshly grated Parmesan

1. Heat some olive oil in a frying pan. Add the sliced leeks and pancetta and sauté over a low heat until the leeks are lightly golden. Add the garlic, celery, carrots and thyme. Cook for 2–3 minutes, stirring occasionally. Pour in the white wine and cook for about 1 minute.
2. Meanwhile, rinse the lentils, then add them to the soup, followed by the stock. Bring to a simmer and check the seasoning, adding salt and pepper if required. Simmer the soup for about 20–30 minutes, or until the lentils are soft.
3. To prepare the Parmesan toasts, brush each side of the ciabatta slices with olive oil. Toast both sides over the grill. Rub one side of the toast with the cut side of the garlic. Sprinkle the Parmesan over and grill again to melt the cheese.

4. To serve, ladle the soup into individual soup bowls and sprinkle the grated Parmesan over. Place some Parmesan toasts on top and serve immediately.

* These Parmesan toasts work with almost all soups or even just as a snack with drinks.

Tuscan Bean Soup with Toasted Garlic

Pasta e fagioli

Serves 4–6

The Tuscans are famous for their variety of soups, most of which came from the peasantry. The origins of most soups were based on frugality and clever, tasty ways of using up leftovers. Ribollita, for example, is a popular soup. It means 'reboiled' and uses beans, pasta, bread and vegetables.

This Tuscan bean soup is a variation of ribollita and I add other ingredients to it depending on what I have available. I particularly like it with fresh baby spinach stirred in at the end (an idea I 'borrowed' from Claudio).

for the Tuscan bean soup:
extra virgin olive oil
1 onion, finely chopped
1 celery stalk, finely diced
1 carrot, finely diced
100g smoked pancetta, diced
2 sprigs of rosemary
1 tbsp tomato purée
1 x 400g tin of mixed Italian beans or beans
   of your choice, drained and rinsed
1 x 400g tin of chopped tomatoes

1 litre chicken stock
75g macaroni
30g freshly grated Parmesan,
   plus extra to serve
salt and freshly ground black pepper
crusty bread, to serve

for the toasted garlic:
6 garlic cloves, sliced
extra virgin olive oil

1. Heat some olive oil in a heavy-based pan. Add in the onion, celery, carrots and pancetta and cook for 10 minutes over a moderate heat. Add in the rosemary, tomato purée, beans, chopped tomatoes and stock. Bring to the boil, then reduce the heat and leave to simmer for 15 minutes.

2. Meanwhile, preheat the oven to 180°C. Place the garlic slices on a well-greased baking tray. Brush the garlic with olive oil and roast for 5 minutes, until golden brown.

3. Remove the rosemary sprigs from the soup and discard. Bring the soup back to the boil and add in the macaroni. Allow to cook for 10–15 minutes, uncovered, or until the pasta is cooked. Remove the pot from the heat, stir in the Parmesan and season.
4. Ladle the soup into bowls. Place roasted garlic slices on top and garnish with grated Parmesan. Serve with crusty bread.

* Cavolo nero is particularly good added to this recipe. Shred it and add it in the last 10 minutes.

Tomato Soup

Zuppa di pomodoro

Serves 6

Another rustic soup, this is as simple as it gets. The bread thickens the soup. I have also had a variation of this recipe in Sicily where rice was used for density instead of the bread.

900g ripe tomatoes or 2 x 400g tins of whole plum tomatoes
2 tbsp extra virgin olive oil
3 garlic cloves, finely chopped
1 small bunch of basil, torn (keep a few leaves for garnish)
2 sprigs of thyme
salt and freshly ground black pepper
sugar, to taste
6 thick slices of day-old ciabatta, crusts removed
1.5 litres chicken stock

1. **If using fresh tomatoes**, peel them by coring the tomatoes, making a cross at the bottom and dipping them into a pot of boiling water for 1 minute. Remove with a slotted spoon, then dip into cold water. The skin will peel off very easily. Cut in half and scoop out all the seeds. Set aside. **If using tinned tomatoes**, roughly chop the tomatoes and push them through a sieve to remove the seeds.
2. Heat the olive oil in a saucepan. Add the garlic and sauté until softened, taking care not to let the garlic brown too much. Add the tomatoes, basil and thyme. Bring to a simmer and season with salt, pepper and sugar to taste. Simmer for about 30 minutes.
3. Tear the bread into chunks and add to the soup. Leave the bread to absorb the tomato flavour for about 1 minute, then add the stock, stirring from time to time. Leave to simmer for about 5 minutes, until the soup has thickened and become more silky in texture. Check the seasoning, adding salt, pepper and sugar as required.
4. To serve, ladle the soup into bowls and garnish with a basil leaf.

✱ For extra zing, I like to spoon a large dollop of pesto into this soup just before serving.

Mussel Soup

Zuppa di cozze

Serves 6

The mussels in this recipe can be replaced with clams. The saffron is optional but does add nicely to the colour and flavour of the dish. For extra richness, stir in some fresh cream at the end.

1kg mussels

extra virgin olive oil

3 garlic cloves, 2 chopped and 1 halved

2 tbsp chopped parsley

½ red chilli, finely chopped

200ml dry white wine

100ml fish stock

200g cherry tomatoes, crushed

pinch of saffron (optional)

12 slices ciabatta

1. To prepare the mussels, rinse them thoroughly in cold water, pull away the beards and discard any open/dead mussels.
2. Heat some olive oil in a large saucepan. Add the chopped garlic and cook for 1 minute, until softened. Add the parsley and chilli and sauté for 2 minutes.
3. Place the cleaned mussels into the saucepan. Add the wine, stock, tomatoes and saffron. Cover the saucepan with a tight-fitting lid and continue to cook for about 5–8 minutes, shaking the saucepan gently from time to time. When all the mussels are open, remove the cut side of the soup from the heat. (If any mussels aren't open at this stage, discard them.)
4. Preheat the grill. Brush the ciabatta slices with olive oil and toast them, then rub with the halved garlic.
5. Ladle the soup into individual bowls and serve with the garlic ciabatta.

✳ When cleaning the mussels, you'll see that some will have opened. Just tap them gently on the work surface and wait a couple of minutes. The fresh ones will close and can be used. Those that remain open should be discarded.

Gnocchi, Polenta, Risotto and Pasta

Gnocchi

Potato Gnocchi with Gorgonzola Sauce
Gnocchi di patate al Gorgonzola

Spinach Gnocchi
Gnocchi verdi

Polenta

Soft Polenta
Polenta morbida

Char-grilled Polenta with Wild Mushroom and Italian Sausage Sauce
Polenta alla griglia con salsa di funghi selvatici e salsiccia

Risotto

Pea and Pesto Risotto
Risotto al pesto e piselli

Roasted Butternut Squash and Sage Risotto with Pine Nuts
Risotto con zucca al forno, salvia e pinoli

Oven-baked Fennel Sausage and Tomato Risotto
Risotto al pomodoro con salsiccia al finocchio

Pasta Making

Plain Pasta

Tomato Pasta

Herb Pasta

Ravioli

Spinach and Ricotta Ravioli
Ravioli di ricotta e spinaci

Butternut Squash Ravioli with Sage and Lemon Butter
Ravioli di zucca con salvia e burro al limone

Pasta

Fresh Pasta Handkerchiefs with Rocket and Pistachio Pesto
Fazzoletti al pesto di rucola e pistacchi

Fresh Farfalle with a Creamy Pancetta and Pea Sauce
Farfalle alla crema con pancetta e piselli

Rigatoni with Aubergine, Tomato, Ricotta Salata and Basil
Pasta alla Norma

Pistachio and Asparagus Penne
Penne agli asparagi e pistacchi

Linguine with Clams
Linguine alla vongole veraci

Tagliatelle with Dublin Bay Prawns and Courgettes
Tagliatelle con gamberoni e zucchine

Spaghetti, Neapolitan Style
Spaghetti alla puttanesca

Spaghetti with Aubergine Balls
Spaghetti con polpette di melanzane

Penne with Vodka Sauce
Penne alla vodka

Spaghetti Carbonara
Spaghetti alla Carbonara

Macaroni Cheese with Mushrooms
Pasticcio al forno con provola, fontina e funghi trifolati

Rigatoni with Sausage and Peppers
Rigatoni con salsiccia e peperoni

Spaghetti with Squid Ink
Spaghetti al nero di seppia

Fettuccine Alfredo

Pasta with Sardines and Wild Fennel
Pasta con le sarde e finocchietto selratico

Lasagne with a Ricotta and Parmesan Sauce
Lasagne alla ricotta e Parmigiano

Gnocchi

Gnocchi are more typical in northern Italy and are usually made with either semolina flour or potato. The word *gnocco* means 'little lump'. They are often sold in a vacuum pack in delicatessens and larger supermarkets. However, they are very easy to make at home and are delicious as a starter. I particularly like the potato gnocchi.

Potato Gnocchi with Gorgonzola Sauce

Gnocchi di patate al Gorgonzola

Serves 6

Gnocchi can handle a good strong sauce and I like this Gorgonzola sauce, which is very rich. It needs to be served immediately, so be ready with the gnocchi.

for the potato gnocchi:
1kg potatoes, unpeeled – use a floury potato
    such as King Edward or Rooster
salt and freshly ground black pepper
1 egg, beaten
300g Italian '00' or strong white flour

for the Gorgonzola sauce:
250ml cream
100g Gorgonzola cheese
salt and freshly ground black pepper
2 tbsp freshly grated Parmesan
1 tsp chopped dill

1. To make the gnocchi, place the unpeeled potatoes in a pot of cold water and bring to the boil. Allow to cook for about 20 minutes, until they are soft in the centre. Remove from the pot and peel the skins while still hot.
2. Mash the potatoes and add 2 large pinches of salt and pepper. Taste for seasoning and adjust accordingly, then add the egg. Mix quickly to prevent the egg from cooking. Add half the flour to the potato mixture and mix thoroughly.

3. Sprinkle the rest of the flour on the work surface and knead the potato mixture until the dough is pliable. Divide the dough into 8 pieces. Using your fingertips, roll out each portion until it's about 2cm thick. Cut each of the 8 rolls into 2cm diagonal pieces and place on a floured tray. Space them evenly to prevent sticking.
4. Bring a pot of water to the boil with 2 tbsp salt. Add the gnocchi and stir gently. When they're done, the gnocchi should float to the top after about 2 ½–3 minutes.
5. While the gnocchi is cooking, you can get on with making the sauce. Bring the cream to a low boil in a saucepan large enough to eventually hold the cooked gnocchi. Remove from the heat and add the remaining ingredients. Stir until the sauce thickens slightly. Check for seasoning. Using a slotted spoon, transfer the cooked gnocchi to the sauce and stir to coat. Serve immediately.

✳ While working with gnocchi, dust your hands often with flour to prevent sticking.

✳ For additional flavour, add 1/4 tsp paprika to the sauce. This sauce is also great as a dip with crudités of carrots and celery.

Spinach Gnocchi

Gnocchi verdi

Serves 6

This is a tasty and colourful variation on the potato gnocchi (p. 80). It takes a little longer to prepare but is worth the trouble. Try it with the Gorgonzola sauce (p. 80) or simply some melted butter, grated Parmesan, a squeeze of lemon juice and salt and pepper.

450g spinach leaves
1kg potatoes, unpeeled – use a floury potato such as King Edward or Rooster
1 egg, beaten
300g Italian '00' or strong white flour
salt and freshly ground black pepper

1. Wilt the spinach in a large saucepan with a little water. Keep stirring, as this will only take a minute. Drain in a colander and squeeze out the excess liquid. Allow to cool.
2. Place the unpeeled potatoes in a pot of cold water and bring to the boil. Allow to cook for about 20 minutes, until they are soft in the centre. Remove from the pot and peel the skins while still hot.
3. Mash the potatoes and add 2 large pinches of salt and pepper. Taste for seasoning and adjust accordingly, then add the egg. Mix quickly to prevent the egg from cooking. Add the spinach and half the flour to the potato mixture and mix thoroughly.
4. Sprinkle the rest of the flour on the work surface and knead the potato and spinach mixture until the dough is pliable. Divide the dough into 8 pieces. Using your fingertips, roll out each portion until it's about 2cm thick. Cut each of the 8 rolls into 2cm diagonal pieces and place on a floured tray. Space them evenly to prevent sticking.
5. Bring a pot of water to boil with 2 tbsp salt. Add the gnocchi and stir gently. When they're done, the gnocchi should float to the top after about 2 ½–3 minutes. Using a slotted spoon, transfer the gnocchi to the sauce.

* These are also delicious added to a vegetable broth soup.
The spinach can be replaced with sun-dried tomato purée for a lovely red gnocchi.

Polenta

Polenta, also known as cornmeal, is a warm, comforting dish that's generally associated with the north of Italy. In fact, it's even more popular than pasta in some areas. It was originally peasant food and has made a huge comeback into the kitchens of Italy in the last four decades.

As a dish, polenta can be prepared soft, which is best with stews, or it can be formed in a block and left to solidify and later grilled on a char-grill pan and served with a sauce.

Soft Polenta

Polenta morbida

Serves 8

1.5 litres water
1½ tsp coarse sea salt
300g polenta (cornmeal)

150g butter
100g freshly grated Parmesan
salt and freshly ground black pepper

1. Pour the water and salt into a large, heavy-based saucepan and bring to the boil. Gradually pour in the polenta while whisking continuously and quickly to ensure the mixture stays smooth and that no lumps form. Add in the butter and Parmesan. (If the polenta does become lumpy during cooking, pour it into a blender and process until smooth, then return it to the pan and continue cooking.)
2. Reduce the heat to its lowest setting and cook for 5 minutes, or until the mixture is thick and creamy and coming away from the pan. Occasionally whisk the mixture to prevent a skin from forming. Season to taste and serve immediately.

✳ Believe me, serve this immediately. The polenta becomes stodgy quite quickly. If that happens, add some hot water or chicken stock and stir very well to ensure there are no lumps.

Char-grilled Polenta with Wild Mushroom and Italian Sausage Sauce

Polenta alla griglia con salsa di funghi selvatici e salsiccia

Serves 4–6

This is really a starter and is wonderful in the autumn and winter. Being a mushroom fan, of course I'm going to say that this sauce is yummy. But it really is delicious and it works well with chicken or pork too, or even as a pasta sauce with some extra cream and stock added. This polenta could also be served with a Gorgonzola sauce (p. 80).

for the char-grilled polenta (makes 12 slices):
1 litre water
1 tsp coarse sea salt
250g polenta (cornmeal)
50g butter
50g freshly grated Parmesan

for the wild mushroom and Italian sausage sauce:
extra virgin olive oil
3 good-quality Italian sausages, chopped
knob of butter
200g wild mushrooms or your favourite selection, sliced thinly
2 garlic cloves, finely chopped
2 tbsp Marsala or sweet sherry
100ml cream
salt and freshly ground black pepper
2 tbsp chopped parsley

1. To make the polenta, pour the water and salt into a large, heavy-based saucepan and bring to the boil. Gradually pour in the polenta while whisking continuously and quickly to ensure the mixture stays smooth and that no lumps form. Add in the butter and

Parmesan. (If the polenta does become lumpy during cooking, pour it into a blender and process until smooth, then return it to the pan and continue cooking.)

2. Reduce the heat to its lowest setting and cook for 5 minutes, or until the mixture is thick and creamy and coming away from the pan. Occasionally whisk the mixture to prevent a skin from forming.
3. Line a loaf tin with cling film and pour in the polenta. Cover the top with cling film and allow to cool and set in the fridge for a minimum of 2 hours.
4. Meanwhile, to make the sauce, heat some oil in a frying pan. Add the chopped sausage and sauté for 5 minutes, until fully cooked. Remove the sausage from the pan and set aside.
5. Add a knob of butter to the pan, then the mushrooms and garlic and sauté on a high heat, stirring constantly, for 4–5 minutes, until the mushrooms are cooked through. Return the sausages to the pan, add the Marsala and cook for 1–2 minutes. Add the cream and warm through for a few minutes. Check the seasoning, adding salt and pepper if necessary. Sprinkle some chopped parsley over and keep warm.
6. Slice the polenta into pieces about 2.5cm thick and fry with a little oil until they are a light golden brown, about 7 minutes. Serve immediately with the mushroom and Italian sausage sauce.

✳ A little secret about cooking mushrooms – if you cook them on a high heat, the juice flows out of the mushrooms. Most people quit at this stage, believing the mushrooms to be ready, but if you continue to stir the mushrooms on the high heat, the juice begins to evaporate and the mushrooms, like sponges, absorb back the now concentrated juice and the result will have everyone begging for more.

✳ I like to fry this polenta on a griddle pan, as the lines formed from the pan look so attractive. In this case, to prevent sticking, I brush the polenta slices with oil before placing them on the pan.

Risotto

'Risotto waits for no man' (or woman, I presume!) is an old Italian saying and it could not be truer. If left sitting for even a few minutes, the al dente risotto rice continues to absorb the creamy sauce and soon it's just a stodgy mess. This puts a lot of people off trying it at home, but in fact, it's all about planning.

They say that once you start preparing risotto you have to see it through, but I have a little trick. I cook off the onions or leeks in advance, add the rice and stir well, add the wine and stir and then I remove it from the heat. When my friends arrive, all I have to do is add the hot stock and stir frequently. The more I stir, the creamier the texture.

Note: There is a variety of risotto rice available, but the best are Arborio, Vialone Nano and Carnaroli. I use Arborio for my risotto and find it very reliable.

Pea and Pesto Risotto

Risotto al pesto e piselli

Serves 4–6

I had this in the lovely Agriturismo Arabesque in Sicily and it came highly recommended by my host for the evening, Francesco Cucuru, who was keen to show me local home-style cooking. In between watching the highlights of the local Palermo soccer match, the chef was only too delighted to share his tip with me, which turned out to be simply stirring a fresh pesto into the risotto at the end. Yum!

1 tbsp extra virgin olive oil
knob of butter
1 onion, finely chopped
1 garlic clove, chopped
400g Arborio rice

150ml white wine
1.5 litres chicken stock, heated to simmering
200g frozen peas, defrosted
25g freshly grated Parmesan
2 tbsp homemade pesto (see pp. 133–6)

1. Heat the olive oil and the knob of butter in a large, heavy-based saucepan. When the butter is foaming, add the onion and cook for 5 minutes, until it's beginning to soften. Add the garlic and rice and cook for a few minutes more, until the rice is shiny and opaque. Add the wine and simmer for 1 minute, stirring constantly. Reduce the heat and add the hot stock a ladleful at a time, stirring constantly until each ladleful is absorbed. Add the peas with the last ladle of stock. The rice should be creamy but still firm to the bite.
2. Remove from the heat and stir in the Parmesan and pesto. Season well. Drizzle with a little olive oil and serve immediately.

✳ Adding about 3 tbsp of cream to a risotto gives an even richer texture. Risotto that has cream added at the end is called a Mantecato.

Roasted Butternut Squash and Sage Risotto with Pine Nuts

Risotto con zucca al forno, salvia e pinoli

Serves 6

This has the wonderful golden orange colours of a risotto milanese *(made with saffron), and the flavour of the butternut works so well with rice. The sprinkling of toasted pine nuts gives a lovely finish to this recipe.*

1 large butternut squash
extra virgin olive oil
2 garlic cloves, chopped
5 sage leaves, finely chopped
sea salt and freshly ground black pepper
3 large knobs of butter, divided
3 leeks, finely sliced

400g Arborio rice
100ml dry white wine
1 litre vegetable stock, heated to simmering
75g pine nuts, to serve
4 tbsp freshly grated Parmesan cheese, plus
   extra for serving

1. Preheat the oven to 200°C.
2. Cut the butternut squash into 6–8 wedges (no need to peel), remove the seeds and place in a roasting tray. Add a generous amount of olive oil, the chopped garlic, half the sage leaves, sea salt and pepper over the butternut squash and rub it in with your hands. Roast in the oven for 40–50 minutes, until softened and golden in colour.
3. Once the squash has cooked, allow it to cool slightly, then scrape the soft flesh away from the skin into a bowl. Mash with a fork or potato masher until it's fairly chunky in texture. Scrape any sticky juices left in the roasting tray into the bowl and keep warm while making the risotto.
4. While the squash is cooking, heat some olive oil and a good knob of butter in a large, heavy-based saucepan. Gently fry the leeks until softened. Add the rice and stir for 1 minute, until the grains are coated with the oil and butter and the rice is shiny and opaque. Add the wine and simmer for 1 minute, stirring constantly. Add a good ladle of hot stock and the remaining sage and season well with salt and pepper. Reduce the heat and add the hot stock a ladleful at a time, stirring constantly until each ladleful is absorbed. After about 15–20 minutes the rice should be creamy but still firm to the bite.

5. Meanwhile, place the pine nuts in a fairly hot dry frying pan and toss around until golden, taking care not to let them burn.

6. Remove the pan from the heat and gently stir the roasted butternut squash into the risotto, along with the Parmesan, the remaining butter and seasoning to taste. Add any extra stock if the risotto seems particularly thick.

7. Spoon the risotto into warmed bowls. Sprinkle with the toasted pine nuts and extra Parmesan and serve immediately.

* There's no need to peel the butternut squash when roasting it. Peeling is so cumbersome, and during the roasting process the skin softens, thereby making it easy to scoop off the flesh once it's roasted.

Oven-baked Fennel Sausage and Tomato Risotto

Risotto al pomodoro con salsiccia al finocchio

Serves 4–6

Following an impromptu invite to cousin Franco's house, his wife Ornella simply put this together and I can still remember the flavours to this day. This risotto won't be creamy, as there is no stirring involved, but it's delicious.

extra virgin olive oil
450g Sicilian fennel sausages
1 onion, chopped
2 garlic cloves, finely sliced
300g Arborio rice
2 celery stalks, finely sliced
1 carrot, finely diced

3 tbsp chopped parsley
750ml chicken stock
100ml dry white wine
1 x 400g tin of cherry tomatoes
salt and freshly ground black pepper

1. Preheat the oven to 180°C.
2. Heat some oil in a casserole dish over a medium heat. Cook the sausages for 15 minutes, until fully cooked. Remove from the dish and slice into bite-sized pieces. Set aside.
3. Add the onion to the dish and sauté on a low heat for 7–10 minutes, until lightly golden. Add the garlic and cook for 1 minute. Add the rice, celery, carrots and parsley. Allow to cook for 2 minutes, stirring from time to time. Return the sausages to the dish.
4. In a separate saucepan, heat the chicken stock, wine and tomatoes, then add to the casserole dish. Season with salt and pepper, stir and cover tightly with foil or a lid.
5. Place in the oven and cook for approximately 45 minutes, until the liquid is absorbed and the rice is just tender, stirring occasionally. Sprinkle with Parmesan shavings and drizzle with some olive oil to serve.

* Try chorizo or one of your favourite local sausages instead of the Sicilian fennel sausages.

Pasta Making

Pasta making is by far the most popular class at our cookery school. I warn students in advance that while the process is simple, it takes time, but the rewards are really worth it. A few important points on pasta making:

✳   For short pasta, use an Italian '00' flour or a strong white flour, but for *pasta lungo* (long pasta), *grano duro* – durum wheat semolina flour – works best as it holds the shape better.

✳   Fresh pasta will cook almost instantly, as soon as it hits the salted water.

✳   Home-made pasta will keep for months when air dried correctly, so make it in batches.

✳   I always suggest to my students that they make flavoured pasta, such as tomato or olive. That way, everyone will know you made it yourself!

✳   It's really important to use good eggs, free-range and organic if possible. This will result in lovely yellow-coloured pasta.

✳   How about a pasta-making party? You make the dough and your guests have fun shaping the pasta before sitting down and enjoying the fruits of their labour.

The following quantities are only guidelines, as depending on the humidity, type of flour, etc. you may need to add a little more flour. The dough must not be too soft – it should be reasonably difficult to knead. Too much extra flour, though, will make the pasta tough and taste floury.

✳ ✳ ✳ ✳ ✳

Plain Pasta

Serves 4

200g Italian '00' flour (or strong white flour) or a blend with *grano duro* flour
pinch of salt
2 medium eggs, free-range and organic if possible
1 tbsp extra virgin olive oil

Tomato Pasta

Serves 4

200g Italian '00' flour (or strong white flour) or a blend with *grano duro* flour
pinch of salt
2 medium eggs, free-range and organic if possible
2 tbsp tomato purée or sun-dried tomato paste (from a tube, not a tin)
Note: For this recipe, blend the salt, eggs and tomato purée before mixing with the flour.

Herb Pasta

Serves 4

200g Italian '00' flour (or strong white flour) or a blend with *grano duro* flour
pinch of salt
2 medium eggs, free-range and organic if possible
3 tbsp chopped fresh herbs
1 tbsp extra virgin olive oil
Note: For this recipe, blend the salt, eggs, herbs and olive oil before mixing with the flour.

Traditional method of making pasta dough

1. Sieve the flour and salt onto a clean work surface and make a well in the centre with your fist. Beat the eggs and oil together and pour them into the well.
2. Gradually mix the liquid ingredients into the flour using the fingers of one hand. Knead the pasta until smooth. Wrap in cling film and allow to rest for at least 30 minutes before rolling it out, as the pasta will be much more elastic after resting.

Making pasta dough in a food processor

1. Add the flour and salt into the bowl of a food processor. Pour in the beaten eggs and oil and process until the dough begins to come together (this will only take a few seconds). Turn out and knead until smooth. Wrap in cling film and rest for at least 30 minutes.

Rolling out using a pasta machine

1. Feed the rested dough through the widest setting several times. Roll the pasta through the machine, narrowing the setting by one notch each time, until the required thickness is reached. As a general guideline, for ravioli, roll to the last (the thinnest) setting. For all other pastas, roll to the second to last setting.
2. For tagliatelle, transfer the dough to the appropriate cutter attachment. Roll the pasta through and hang over a dowel or broom handle.
3. For farfalle, cut the dough into 3cm strips and pinch in the middle to form a bow. Place on a floured tray.

To cook pasta

1. As a guide, you'll need 4 litres of water and 3 tbsp salt for every 350–450g fresh or dried pasta. It's often recommended that 1 tbsp of olive oil will help to stop the water from boiling over and will prevent the pasta from sticking, but if you have enough water in the pot and you stir the pasta as it goes in, it won't stick. Do not cover the pot or the water will boil over.
2. Bring the pasta back to a rolling boil, stir once and cook until al dente. This could take a little as 1–2 minutes for fresh pasta.
3. Quickly drain the pasta well using a large colander or sieve. Hold back 2–3 tbsp of the cooking water and add to the pasta if it's sticking together. Add the pasta immediately to the sauce, extra virgin olive oil or butter. Serve immediately.

Ravioli

Home-made ravioli is truly delicious. In the interest of speed, I usually make large ravioli
and serve 3 or 5 per person. If you're in a real hurry and want to impress, there is also
open ravioli, which in fact are *fazzoletti* (p. 106), with filling between each sheet.

✳ ✳ ✳ ✳ ✳

Spinach and Ricotta Ravioli

Ravioli di ricotta e spinaci

Serves 4–6

Spinach and ricotta work so well together. Not only do I use this filling for ravioli, I also use it as a crêpe or omelette filling, in lasagne or simply spread on lightly toasted ciabatta with some cracked black pepper.

for the pasta:
400g Italian '00' flour (or strong white flour) or a blend with *grano duro* flour
large pinch of salt
4 medium eggs, free-range and organic if possible
2 tbsp extra virgin olive oil

for the filling:
extra virgin olive oil
1 large onion, finely chopped
450g spinach
175g ricotta
½ tsp freshly grated nutmeg
salt and freshly ground black pepper

to finish:
1 egg, beaten
75g butter, melted
25g freshly grated Parmesan
chopped parsley

1. Make the pasta dough as per the instructions on p. 100.
2. While the dough is resting, heat some olive oil in a pan. Sweat the chopped onion on a low heat for 7–10 minutes, until soft. Remove the onion from the oil with a slotted spoon, draining well, and set aside.
3. Sauté the spinach in a large, dry saucepan on a low heat, stirring constantly to prevent it from sticking. Allow to cool, then squeeze it dry by hand or by gently pushing on it in a sieve.
4. To make the filling, place the onion, spinach, ricotta, nutmeg and seasoning in a food processor and blend until smooth. Cover and refrigerate.
5. After the dough has rested, cut it in half. Rewrap one half in cling film. Roll the other out to the finest setting on the pasta machine. Cover with a clean damp tea towel and repeat the process with the remaining dough.

6. Spoon 1 tsp of the filling in even rows on one piece of the dough, spacing them at 6cm intervals. Brush the spaces between the dough very lightly with the beaten egg. Carefully lift up the other half and lay it over the first piece. Press down firmly between the pockets of filling, pushing out any trapped air.
7. Cut into squares using a pastry cutter (or circles using a scone cutter) and transfer to a floured tray.
8. To cook, bring a large pot of water to the boil. Add the ravioli and cook for about 4–5 minutes, until the dough is cooked through. Drain and serve with the melted butter and grated Parmesan and garnish with some chopped parsley.

* It's important to press all the air out of the ravioli before sealing it, otherwise the ravioli will float in the water and won't cook evenly.

Butternut Squash Ravioli with Sage and Lemon Butter

Ravioli di zucca con salvia e burro al limone

Serves 4–6

This ravioli filling is quite sweet, so the lemon and sage butter balances the flavours out. I also use this filling for vegetarian cannelloni.

for the pasta:
400g Italian '00' flour (or strong white flour) or a blend with *grano duro* flour
large pinch of salt
4 medium eggs, free-range and organic if possible
2 tbsp extra virgin olive oil
sage and lemon butter, to serve (p. 137)

for the filling:
450g butternut squash
1 garlic clove
extra virgin olive oil
salt and freshly ground black pepper
2 eggs
25g freshly grated Parmesan, plus extra to serve
25g fresh white breadcrumbs
10g ground almonds
pinch of freshly grated nutmeg

1. Preheat the oven to 200°C.
2. Make the pasta dough as per the instructions on p. 100.
3. To make the filling, cut the butternut squash into 6–8 wedges, remove the seeds and place the pieces in a roasting tray.
4. Pound or chop the garlic and add the olive oil, salt and pepper. Pour it over the butternut squash and rub it in with your hands. Roast in the oven for 30–40 minutes, until softened and golden in colour.

5. Once the squash has cooked, allow it to cool slightly, then scrape the soft flesh away from the skin into a bowl. Mash with a fork or potato masher until smooth. Stir in the yolks of 2 eggs, Parmesan, breadcrumbs, ground almonds and nutmeg and seasoning to taste.

6. After the dough has rested, cut it in half. Rewrap one half in cling film. Roll the other out to the finest setting on the pasta machine. Cover with a clean damp tea towel and repeat the process with the remaining dough.

7. Lightly beat the remaining egg. Spoon 1 tsp of the filling in even rows on one piece of the dough, spacing them at 6cm intervals. Brush the spaces between the dough very lightly with the beaten egg. Carefully lift up the other half and lay it over the first piece. Press down firmly between the pockets of filling, pushing out any trapped air.

8. Cut into squares using a pastry cutter (or circles using a scone cutter), a serrated knife or a special ravioli cutter. Transfer to a floured tray.

9. To cook, bring a large pot of water to the boil. Add the ravioli and cook for about 3–4 minutes (depending on the size of the ravioli), until puffy. Drain.

10. To serve, pour the sage and lemon butter over the ravioli and sprinkle with some freshly grated Parmesan cheese. Serve immediately.

* If you aren't going to eat the ravioli immediately, drop them into the boiling water as you make each batch and cook for just 1 minute, then lift out with a slotted spoon and drop into a bowl of cold water. Drain and lay out on lightly oiled trays, cover with cling film and chill until needed. (They should hold in the refrigerator for 1 day using this method.) Then drop them back into boiling salted water just before serving and cook for 3 minutes.

Pasta

Fresh Pasta Handkerchiefs with Rocket and Pistachio Pesto

Fazzoletti al pesto di rucola e pistacchi

Serves 6

This is the simplest of pasta shapes, just squares or rectangles of pasta. They could also be used for a lasagne dish.

1 x plain pasta dough (p. 98)
extra virgin olive oil
rocket and pistachio pesto (p. 134)
2 tbsp semi-dried cherry tomatoes
freshly grated Parmesan

1. Make the pasta dough as per the instructions on p. 100.
2. Divide the dough into 5 equal pieces. Roll the dough through all the settings on your pasta machine, ending with the second to last setting. Keep the dough you're not working with covered with a damp cloth. Cut the dough into 12cm x 8cm rectangles.
3. Bring a large pot of salted water to the boil. Add a little olive oil. Cook the rectangles for about 2–3 minutes and carefully lift them out with a slotted spoon.
4. Add 2–3 tbsp of the pasta cooking water to the pesto to loosen it.
5. Gently toss the pasta rectangles with the pesto and semi-dried cherry tomatoes. Sprinkle over some grated Parmesan and serve immediately.

Fresh Farfalle with a Creamy Pancetta and Pea Sauce

Farfalle alla crema con pancetta e piselli

Serves 4

This is a type of carbonara, but with peas and pancetta. It's such a fast, simple recipe that I recommend that the pasta is cooked before you start to make the sauce. Do ensure that the pasta is piping hot, though, as it will cook the eggs.

1 x plain pasta recipe (p. 98), shaped into farfalle (see instructions on p. 100)
1 tbsp extra virgin olive oil
150g pancetta, sliced
6 egg yolks
100g freshly grated Pecorino cheese (or Parmesan and Pecorino mixed),
    plus extra for serving
salt and freshly ground black pepper
150g peas, lightly precooked

1. Cook the farfalle in boiling salted water. When the pasta is ready, drain and reserve some of the cooking liquid.
2. Meanwhile, heat the olive oil in a large frying pan. Fry the pancetta until cooked and slightly crispy. Set aside on kitchen paper and drain the excess oil from the frying pan.
3. Beat the egg yolks with the cheese and season with salt and pepper.
4. Add the pancetta back to the hot pan, along with the peas. Tip the pasta into the frying pan, adding a ladleful of the reserved cooking liquid from the pasta. Pour over the egg mixture, stirring to coat each piece of pasta.
5. Sprinkle over extra cheese and black pepper to taste and serve.

* Almost any pasta will work with this recipe. The peas can be replaced with grated courgettes, blanched asparagus or baby spinach.

Rigatoni with Aubergine, Tomato, Ricotta Salata and Basil

Pasta alla Norma

Serves 4

I'm on a mission to convert everyone to enjoying aubergines. Sicilians love their aubergines and incorporate them into almost every part of their meal, except dessert. In this recipe, the aubergines add a wonderful silkiness to the pasta dish, which was called after the famous opera, Norma, *composed by Bellini from Catania in Sicily. It's said that Bellini enjoyed* Melanzane alla Parmigiana *(p. 12) so much that his local restaurant created this pasta dish for him.*

3 medium aubergines, finely sliced
60g salt
500ml extra virgin olive oil
800g tomato sauce (p. 130)

300–375g rigatoni
salt and freshly ground black pepper
basil leaves, for garnish
90g ricotta salata

1. Degorge the aubergines by placing the slices in a colander and sprinkling with the salt. Leave for 15 minutes to allow the bitter juices to drain, then rinse the aubergines and pat dry.
2. Fry the aubergines in the olive oil in batches until they're soft and golden. Set aside and keep warm.
3. Pour the tomato sauce into a saucepan and heat through, keeping warm.
4. Meanwhile, cook the rigatoni as per the packet instructions. The pasta should be al dente, with a bite – remember, the pasta will continue to cook a little in the next stage of this recipe. Drain the pasta, reserving some of the cooking liquid.
5. In a separate pan, add the pasta into the heated tomato sauce. If the pasta is a little sticky, loosen it with the reserved cooking liquid. Taste for seasoning.
6. Transfer to a serving platter, spoon over any remaining sauce and place the aubergines on top. Shred some basil on top and grate the ricotta salata over. Drizzle with a little extra virgin olive oil and serve.

✳ Rigatoni is best with this dish, but if unavailable, try large penne. Ricotta salata is a hard, salted ricotta cheese. If unavailable, try feta.

109

Pistachio and Asparagus Penne

Penne agli asparagi e pistacchi

Serves 4

The Nebrodi Mountain farmers are famous for their Sicilian black pigs, hazelnuts and pistachios, among other things. I was fortunate enough to enjoy a wonderful meal in a lovely mountainside restaurant near Bronte, where I sampled three pasta dishes with pistachios as a key ingredient, then finished the meal with a pistachio cake and pistachio ice cream.

You might think it strange to sprinkle dried breadcrumbs over pasta, but they were used in Sicily as the poor man's Parmesan. Nowadays, they are firmly part of the food culture and work really well. I always feel that I have to explain that to my guests when serving the breadcrumbs and no Parmesan, just in case they think I'm being downright mean!

extra virgin olive oil
35g breadcrumbs
350g asparagus, cut into 2cm pieces
300–375g penne
100g pancetta, diced
1 red pepper, deseeded and finely chopped

2 tsp chopped thyme
2 garlic cloves, chopped
400ml cream
30g black olives, pitted and halved
50g pistachio nuts, chopped
salt and freshly ground black pepper

1. Heat about 2 tbsp olive oil in a frying pan and sauté the breadcrumbs until brown. Drain on kitchen paper and set aside.
2. Blanch the asparagus in simmering water for about 2 minutes, depending on the thickness of the stems, until just al dente. Drain and refresh in ice-cold water to retain the colour.
3. Cook the pasta as per the packet instructions.
4. Heat a little oil in a frying pan, then cook the pancetta, red pepper and thyme for 2 minutes. Add the garlic and cook for another 30 seconds. Add the asparagus and cook over a high heat for 2 minutes. Pour in the cream and warm through. Drain the pasta and stir it into the sauce.
5. Divide the pasta onto serving plates. Sprinkle with the olives, chopped pistachio and bread-crumbs. Check for seasoning, adding salt and pepper as required. Serve immediately.

* For a vegetarian version, replace the pancetta with sliced chestnut mushrooms.

Linguine with Clams

Linguine alla vongole veraci

Serves 4–6

As pasta dishes go, this has to be my husband's favourite – after pasta con le sarde, and pasta with squid ink sauce, and ... well, he simply loves pasta. Vongole veraci are known as carpet shell clams. They are common Sicilian clams, but any clams will work in this recipe.

1 ½kg clams
extra virgin olive oil
2 garlic cloves, chopped
1 bunch of parsley, finely chopped
100ml good Italian white wine
300–375g small linguine or spaghetti
salt and freshly ground black pepper

1. Clean the clams thoroughly and discard any open clams.
2. Heat a little olive oil in a frying pan. Sauté the garlic and most of the parsley. Add the clams, then pour in the white wine and cover with a lid. Continue to cook and shake the pan from time to time for 2–3 minutes, until the clams open. (Discard any clams that are still closed.) Uncover and allow the liquid to reduce slightly.
3. Meanwhile, cook the pasta according to the packet instructions. Drain in a colander.
4. Add the pasta to the clams. Add the rest of the chopped parsley and stir. Add 1 tbsp olive oil and seasoning to taste.

* Clams tend to catch sand in their shells, so a few good rinses in cold water should wash out all the sand. Any open clams should be tapped on a hard surface. If they close, then they're safe to eat, otherwise discard them. Similarly, discard any cracked or broken ones and any that don't open during the cooking process.

Tagliatelle with Dublin Bay Prawns and Courgettes

Tagliatelle con gamberoni e zucchine

Serves 4

La Sirinella is our local restaurant in Sicily. The food there is so good that we telephone in our order when our plane lands in Trapani airport. Then Claudio drives like a local (ahem!), our mouths watering in anticipation of their pasta dishes. This is my version of their best. I tried so hard to get the recipe from their chef but he wouldn't budge.

36 Dublin Bay prawns
salt and freshly ground black pepper
extra virgin olive oil
1 tbsp chopped fresh parsley
300–375g tagliatelle
2 medium courgettes, grated

1 anchovy, chopped
1 large garlic clove, chopped
1 large red chilli, diced
80ml dry white wine
1 x 400g tin of cherry tomatoes
juice of 1 lemon

1. Remove the heads and tails of 32 Dublin Bay prawns and devein them as well. Slice the remaining 4 prawns in half and devein them. Place the 4 halved prawns on a grill rack, flesh side up, and season with salt, pepper, extra virgin olive oil and parsley. Set aside.
2. Cook the tagliatelle as per the packet instructions.
3. Meanwhile, heat a little olive oil in a frying pan. Lightly sauté the 32 prawns for about 4 minutes, or until cooked. Remove and set aside.
4. Add the courgettes, anchovy, garlic and chilli to the hot pan and cook lightly for 3–4 minutes. Pour over the white wine and cook for a few minutes. Add the cherry tomatoes and heat through, lightly crushing the tomatoes with the back of a wooden spoon. Add the prawns back in and season with salt and pepper (and maybe a pinch of sugar).
5. Meanwhile, grill the remaining 4 prawns (8 halves) and finish with a squeeze of lemon juice.
6. Drain the tagliatelle and add it to the sauce. Arrange on a serving platter and place the halved Dublin Bay prawns on top.

* Add some cream to the sauce for a richer finish.

Spaghetti, Neapolitan Style

Spaghetti alla puttanesca

Serves 4

I always believed that this recipe had its origins in Naples, only to be told recently that the people of Syracuse in Sicily also lay claim to it. One thing for sure is the interesting title, which when politely translated means spaghetti for the 'lady of the night'. It's fiery, spicy and salty, so adjust the quantity of dried chilli flakes according to the level of tolerance of your taste buds.

extra virgin olive oil
1 garlic clove, minced
1 x 400g tin of chopped tomatoes
salt and freshly ground black pepper
½ tsp crushed chilli flakes
   (less if your prefer less heat)

1 tbsp chopped parsley
1 tsp dried oregano
300–375g spaghetti or vermicelli
2 anchovy fillets, chopped
2 tbsp capers, chopped
8 black olives, pitted and sliced

1. Heat a little olive oil in a heavy-based frying pan, then sauté the garlic until it's lightly coloured. Add the tomatoes, salt and pepper to taste. Add the chilli flakes and cook the mixture over a medium heat for 3–4 minutes, until the tomato liquid is slightly reduced. Lower the heat, add the parsley and oregano and simmer the sauce gently for 30 minutes.
2. Meanwhile, cook the pasta until it's al dente.
3. Mash the anchovies with a fork and add them, the capers and the olives to the pan. Continue cooking the sauce over a low heat until the pasta is ready.
4. Drain the cooked pasta and toss it with the sauce. Serve hot.

✳ Be prepared to add a little sugar if the tinned
   tomatoes are acidic.

Spaghetti with Aubergine Balls

Spaghetti con polpette di melanzane

Serves 4

This is apparently the 'poor man's meatballs', but there is nothing poor about this dish. The roasted aubergines, mashed and mixed with the breadcrumbs and seasoning, form the softest, lightest meatballs ever. I first dubiously tried this at a family gathering in a lovely restaurant, Trattoria ai Cascinari, in Palermo and was immediately converted. I actually prefer this to real meatballs. The trick is to keep the aubergine balls light and not compact them too much.

2 large aubergines
extra virgin olive oil
salt and freshly ground black pepper
200g breadcrumbs (you may need more,
    depending on the size of the aubergines)
4 large garlic cloves, finely chopped
125g freshly grated Pecorino

2 tsp chopped mint
1 tsp dried oregano
2 egg yolks
pinch of nutmeg
500ml tomato sauce (p. 130)
300–375g spaghetti
ricotta salata, to serve

1. Preheat the oven to 180°C.
2. Cut the aubergines in half, then rub them with oil and sprinkle with salt and pepper. Place on a baking tray and roast for about 30 minutes. Allow to cool slightly, then scoop out the flesh and place in a sieve to squeeze out the excess liquid. Mash the garlic with the aubergine flesh.
3. Combine the breadcrumbs with the grated Pecorino, mint, oregano, egg yolks and nutmeg. Add the aubergine flesh and salt and pepper to taste. Mould the mixture into balls about the size of golf balls.
4. Heat some olive oil in a frying pan. Fry one small ball first, then taste and test for the correct seasoning. Fry off the remaining balls in 2 batches, until golden, turning from time to time and taking care not to crowd the pan. Place on kitchen paper to drain.
5. Pour off the oil from the pan, lower the heat and add the tomato sauce. Add the balls to the sauce and simmer gently in the sauce for 10–15 minutes.
6. Meanwhile, cook the spaghetti as per the packet instructions. Drain and serve with the *polpette* and tomato sauce with some ricotta salata grated over.

✱ Grated cheese enhances this dish, so if ricotta salata is
unavailable, try Parmesan.

Penne with Vodka Sauce

Penne alla vodka

Serves 4

Vodka and pasta may seem like an odd combination, but in my travels in Rome, I was blown away by this delicious dish. Apparently the Russians, who were trying to increase the vodka sales in the restaurants in the city, were offering incentives, so what did the canny chefs do but add it to a pasta sauce. Well, that's one way of boosting sales.

300g penne
1 tbsp extra virgin olive oil
1 ½ red chillies
2 tbsp tomato purée
60ml tbsp water
250ml double cream
60ml tbsp vodka
75g freshly grated Parmesan
salt and freshly ground black pepper

1. Cook the pasta according to the packet instructions.
2. Heat the olive oil in a large frying pan that's big enough to also hold the cooked pasta. Add the chillies and sauté over a medium heat for 1–2 minutes. Add the tomato purée and the water.
3. Simmer over a low heat for 1–2 minutes, stirring frequently with a wooden spoon to prevent it from sticking to the pan and burning. If need be, add more water.
4. Stir the cream into the chilli and tomato mixture. Add the vodka and simmer for about 3 minutes more.
5. Drain the pasta and transfer to the pan with the sauce, then add the Parmesan cheese. Mix thoroughly, taste for seasoning and transfer to a warm bowl.

✳ For a twist, add smoked salmon or cooked prawns at the last minute and heat through.

Spaghetti Carbonara

Spaghetti alla Carbonara

Serves 4–6

A Roman dish but known worldwide, this dish is easy, yummy and more-ish. The Romans are so proud of their creation that they have a 'Carbonara Club' and only the best chefs are allowed in.

Real carbonara doesn't contain cream. The eggs mix with the pasta cooking liquid form a creamy, silky sauce.

300g spaghetti
120g pancetta, cut into 1–1 ½ cm dice
4 egg yolks, beaten
100g freshly grated Pecorino Romano
freshly ground black pepper

1. Cook the pasta according to the packet instructions.
2. Meanwhile, heat a frying pan and sauté the pancetta until golden brown. Drain on kitchen paper and set aside.
3. Combine the egg yolks, most of the cheese and some pepper in a large bowl. Drain the pasta, reserving some of the cooking liquid. Add about 200ml of the cooking liquid to the eggs and whisk together.
4. Tip the spaghetti into the pan. Add the pancetta, toss in the egg mix and heat gently. The eggs will emulsify to a creamy sauce.
5. To serve, add the remaining cheese and more black pepper.

Macaroni Cheese with Mushrooms

Pasticcio al forno con provola, fontina e funghi trifolati

Serves 4

Macaroni cheese might seem old-fashioned and uninteresting, but introducing the Provolone and Fontina lifts this dish to new heights. That said, as an Irish farmer's daughter, I never object to this recipe made with locally farm-produced strong cheddar.

300–375g macaroni pasta
3 tbsp extra virgin olive oil
225g button mushrooms, sliced
1 garlic clove, finely sliced
2 sprigs of thyme
2 tbsp butter
4 tbsp plain flour
600ml milk

½ tsp Dijon mustard
90g grated Provolone cheese
90g grated Fontina cheese
salt and freshly ground black pepper
a knob of butter, for greasing
25g breadcrumbs
20g grated Pecorino cheese
2 tbsp finely chopped flat-leaf parsley

1. Preheat the oven to 180°C and butter a large gratin dish.
2. Cook the macaroni in plenty of boiling salted water according to the packet instructions.
3. Heat the oil in a large saucepan. Add the mushrooms, garlic and thyme and cook gently for 2–3 minutes. Remove the garlic mushrooms and set aside.
4. Melt the butter in the saucepan. Stir in the flour until it's blended with the butter, add the milk and keep stirring. Add the mustard and grated Provolone and Fontina. Season with salt and pepper. Allow to simmer for 2–3 minutes, stirring constantly, until the sauce has thickened.
5. Drain the macaroni and mix with the sauce. Stir in the mushrooms, then pour the macaroni and cheese mixture into the prepared dish.
6. Mix the breadcrumbs, Pecorino and parsley together and scatter over the macaroni cheese. Bake for 15–20 minutes, until golden brown and bubbling.

✳ Replace the Provolone and Fontina with grated Parmesan and Gruyère - it works beautifully. I also put a layer of baby spinach in the centre, which is lovely for colour and flavour.

Rigatoni with Sausage and Peppers

Rigatoni con salsiccia e peperoni

Serves 6 Ⓔ Ⓕ

This is a nice, easy family supper. It's possible to replace the Italian sausages with 200g chorizo should there be a family aversion to fennel.

extra virgin olive oil
1 onion, chopped
2 red peppers, sliced
2 yellow peppers, sliced
1 red chilli, finely chopped
2 large garlic cloves, finely chopped
½ tsp fennel seeds
150ml white wine

250ml chicken stock
450g rigatoni
400g good-quality Italian sausages, casings
   removed and cut into 1–1 ½cm pieces
salt and freshly ground black pepper
fresh chopped parsley, to serve
freshly grated Parmesan, to serve

1. Heat a little oil in a frying pan and sauté the onions, peppers and chilli on a low heat for about 5–8 minutes, until softened. Add the garlic and fennel seeds and sauté for 1 minute. Add the wine and cook for 1–2 minutes, until the alcohol has cooked off. Add the stock and simmer for about 10 minutes.
2. Cook the pasta according to the packet instructions, until al dente.
3. Meanwhile, heat some oil in a separate pan, then fry the sausages until browned and cooked through. Add the sausages and the drained pasta to the sauce and stir to combine, allowing the pasta to absorb some of the sauce. Season with salt and pepper to taste. Serve immediately, garnishing with parsley and a little grated Parmesan cheese.

∗ A tubular pasta works well with this sauce, so if rigatoni is unavailable, try penne.

Spaghetti with Squid Ink

Spaghetti al nero di seppia

Serves 4

It's possible to buy squid ink pasta, which is totally black in colour, and serve this with a sauce of your choice, usually a fish-based sauce. This recipe is typical Sicilian, and in this case, the sauce is blackened by the squid ink and the pasta is regular pasta. When purchasing the squid, check that the ink sac is intact, otherwise it won't be possible to continue with the recipe. I purchase sachets of condensed squid ink when in Sicily, as it's available in every supermarket.

650g fresh whole squid, uncleaned (with ink sac intact)
3 tbsp extra virgin olive oil
2 garlic cloves, chopped
60ml dry white wine
1 small bunch parsley, chopped
salt and freshly ground black pepper
300–375g spaghetti
freshly grated Parmesan, to serve

1. Begin by cleaning the squid: carefully separate the heads with their tentacles, then remove the guts, setting aside the ink sacs (be careful not to break them). Wash the squid well under cold water. Dice the bodies and chop the tentacles and set aside. Open the ink sacs and collect the ink in a bowl.
2. Heat the oil in a pot and gently sauté the garlic for 1 minute. Add the white wine and simmer for about 2 minutes, until the alcohol has cooked off. Add the squid ink and simmer over a low heat for about 45 minutes, checking that it's not sticking (add a little hot water if it does). Add the squid, chopped parsley and freshly ground black pepper and simmer for 10 minutes more. At this point the sauce should be neither soupy nor too dry (add hot water if required).
3. Cook the pasta according to the packet instructions, until al dente. Drain and add it to the squid ink sauce and stir well, allowing the pasta to absorb some of the sauce and turn black. Check for seasoning and serve with freshly grated Parmesan.

* Some cooks add tomato purée to this recipe for depth of colour and flavour.

123

Fettuccine Alfredo

Serves 4 **E**

I had the pleasure of enjoying this dish at its source in Rome. Alfredo alla Scrofa developed this recipe for its movie star clients in the 1950s. To impress, he mixed the pasta and the other ingredients at the table using a gold fork and spoon. It's simply a pasta dish made from fettuccine tossed with Parmesan cheese and butter. As the cheese melts, it emulsifies the liquids to form a smooth, rich coating on the pasta.

300–375g fettuccine
250ml double cream
30g butter
salt and freshly ground black pepper
grating of fresh nutmeg
100g freshly grated Parmesan

1. Cook the fettuccine according to the packet directions.
2. Meanwhile, bring the cream and butter to a boil in a saucepan large enough to eventually hold the cooked fettuccine. Reduce the heat to low and add the salt, pepper and nutmeg.
3. As soon as it's ready, drain the fettuccine and toss it in the sauce. Add the Parmesan and toss until the fettuccine is well coated and the sauce has thickened. Check for seasoning, adding additional salt and pepper and/or grated Parmesan and serve immediately.

* Outside of Italy, this dish is sometimes served with other ingredients, such as garlic, broccoli, asparagus, prawns or chicken.

* The original recipe calls for only butter and grated cheese. To 'lighten' the dish, I've added cream and reduced the amount of butter.

Pasta with Sardines and Wild Fennel

Pasta con le sarde e finocchietto selratico

Serves 4

I don't think I've ever been in any local restaurant in Sicily that didn't offer this dish, and every home has their own recipe too. This is an interesting recipe, as it's an example of all the good Sicilian ingredients, such as sardines and wild fennel, but it also shows the Arab influence, such as the sweet raisins and pine nuts. It's best made with fresh sardines, but use tinned if there is no alternative.

100ml dry white wine
pinch of saffron
3 tbsp golden raisins (the smaller, the better)
extra virgin olive oil
1 fennel bulb, trimmed and very thinly sliced, fronds chopped and reserved for garnish
1 onion, finely diced
1 tsp fennel seeds, ground in a pestle and mortar
2 anchovy fillets or 1 tsp anchovy paste
2 large fresh sardines, skinned and pinned, or 2 tins of sardines in olive oil, drained
4 tbsp pine nuts
100g fine breadcrumbs
300–375g bucatini (pasta)
1 sprig parsley, chopped, for garnish

1. Gently warm the wine with the saffron and the raisins, then remove from the heat and leave for the flavours to infuse.
2. Meanwhile, heat some olive oil in large frying pan over a medium heat. Add the sliced fennel, onion and fennel seeds and cook, stirring, for 5–7 minutes, until the fennel and onion begin to soften. Add the anchovy fillets (or anchovy paste) to the pan and crush into a paste with the back of a spoon, then stir into the fennel and onion. Pour in the wine mix and bring to a simmer to cook off the alcohol. Chop the sardines and add them to the pan. Lower the heat and simmer for about 10–15 minutes.

3. Meanwhile, toast the pine nuts for about 4 minutes in a dry frying pan, until golden, and set aside. Then toast the breadcrumbs in the same pan, stirring all the time. As soon as they are ready, remove them from the heat and stir in 2 tbsp extra virgin olive oil. Set aside.
4. Cook the pasta according to the packet instructions.
5. Add the drained pasta to the sauce, along with the toasted pine nuts, the fennel fronds and salt and pepper to taste.
6. To serve, top with the toasted breadcrumbs and garnish with the parsley.

* This recipe is traditionally made with bucatini, which is tubular, hollow pasta. If unavailable, use spaghetti. Use caution with salt for seasoning if using the anchovy paste, as this will add salt to the recipe.

Lasagne with a Ricotta and Parmesan Sauce

Lasagne alla ricotta e Parmigiano

Serves 6

Lasagne should be moist, rich and creamy. That said, I find béchamel sauce too rich, so I replace it with a delicious (and very simple) ricotta and Parmesan sauce.

for the ragù:
2 tbsp extra virgin olive oil
2 celery stalks, finely chopped
2 carrots, finely diced
1 red onion, chopped
2 garlic cloves, crushed
1 sprig of rosemary
700g lean minced beef
100ml red wine
200ml beef stock
600g canned chopped tomatoes

1 tbsp tomato purée
salt and freshly ground
   black pepper

for the ricotta and Parmesan sauce:
2 eggs
200g ricotta cheese
200ml cream
70g freshly grated
   Parmesan cheese

¼ tsp grated nutmeg
salt and freshly ground black
   pepper

for the lasagne:
150g mozzarella, thinly sliced
10 basil leaves
9 lasagne sheets
40g freshly grated Parmesan
salt and freshly ground black
   pepper

1. To prepare the ragù sauce, heat the olive oil in a large saucepan and sauté the celery, carrots and onion for about 10 minutes, until soft. Add the garlic and rosemary and cook for 1 minute more.
2. Add the beef and brown on a high heat, then pour over the wine and cook for 2–3 minutes. Add the stock, tomatoes and tomato purée and season with salt and pepper. Simmer uncovered for 35–45 minutes. You may need to add a little more stock and check the seasoning, adding more salt and pepper to taste.
3. Meanwhile, preheat the oven to 180°C.
4. To prepare the ricotta sauce, beat the eggs in a large bowl, then add the ricotta, cream, Parmesan, nutmeg and salt and pepper, stirring until well combined.
5. To assemble, grease a 30cm x 20cm lasagne dish. Begin the layers with ragù sauce, then 3 lasagne sheets, followed by mozzarella slices, basil, 3 lasagne sheets and the ricotta sauce. Repeat the layers, ending with the ricotta sauce. Sprinkle with the grated Parmesan and bake for 30–35 minutes, or until golden brown.

✳ Try making this with homemade fresh pasta (p. 98) for delicious results.

127

Sauces and Pesto

Tomato Sauce
Salsa di pomodoro

Spicy Tomato Sauce
Arrabbiata

Trapanese Pesto with Fresh Tomatoes
and Almonds
Pesto Trapanese

Rocket and Pistachio Pesto
Pesto di rucola e pistacchi

Walnut Pesto
Pesto di noci

Sage and Lemon Butter
Burro alla salvia e limone

Tomato Sauce

Salsa di pomodoro

Makes 750ml

This is a core recipe in Italian cuisine. I usually make it in huge batches and freeze it. It's so versatile that I use it with pasta, on pizzas, in lasagne, as a soup and also with fish and chicken. I just add additional herbs, fresh chillies and spices to suit the dish.

50ml extra virgin olive oil
3 garlic cloves, finely chopped
1 tsp tomato purée
2 x 400g tins of whole plum tomatoes, crushed
salt and freshly ground black pepper
sugar
10 large fresh basil leaves

1. Heat the olive oil in a large pan. Add the garlic and cook for about 2–3 minutes on a low heat, until soft. Add the tomato purée and cook for a further 1 minute. Add the tomatoes along with their juice and season with salt and pepper. Bring to the boil, reduce the heat and simmer for about 30 minutes, or until the sauce has thickened. Adjust the salt, pepper and sugar as necessary. At the last minute, shred the basil and add to the sauce.
2. This sauce will keep in the fridge for 1 week and can be frozen for months.

* In the height of the summer, when I have lovely ripe, red, juicy tomatoes, I make this sauce in bulk, but good-quality tins of plum tomatoes or jars of passata are equally as good.

Spicy Tomato Sauce

Arrabbiata

Makes 350ml

Those that like heat will certainly enjoy this sauce. The chilli flakes give this dish its name –
arribbiata means 'angry style', as in turning red with anger. It's best served with tubular
pasta such as penne, which will hold the sauce. To tone the sauce down, fresh red chillies
are a softer blow than chilli flakes.

extra virgin olive oil
1 onion, finely chopped
3 garlic cloves, chopped
100ml white wine
1 x 400g tin of cherry tomatoes
2 tbsp tomato purée

1 tbsp lemon juice
1 ½ tsp chilli flakes (or to taste)
salt, pepper and sugar
2 tbsp chopped parsley
3 tbsp chopped basil

1. Heat some oil in a saucepan. Add the onion and sauté on a low heat for 7–10 minutes,
    until soft. Add the garlic and sauté for 1 minute, then add the white wine and simmer
    for 2 minutes. Add the cherry tomatoes, tomato purée, lemon juice and chilli flakes.
    Bring to a simmer and cook for 30 minutes. Add salt, pepper and sugar to taste,
    followed by the parsley and basil. Serve with grated Parmesan or Pecorino sprinkled
    over.
2. This sauce will keep in the fridge for 1 week and can be frozen for months.

* To get the best out of the cherry tomatoes, crush them with
   the back of a wooden spoon when they're in the saucepan,
   thereby bursting the fruit open.

Trapanese Pesto with Fresh Tomatoes and Almonds

Pesto Trapanese

Makes 250ml

The 'Trapanese' is from Trapani in Sicily, where the Arabs introduced almonds into the cuisine. It's our family favourite, as the almonds are so unusual. The best pesto is made by hand using a pestle and mortar. The flavours meld together as they are pounded with the pestle and the resulting texture is much better than that from a food processor.

125g blanched almonds
2 garlic cloves
50g fresh basil leaves
200ml extra virgin olive oil
3 ripe tomatoes, 10 ripe cherry tomatoes or ½ x 400g tin of cherry tomatoes
1 tsp sugar
salt and freshly ground black pepper

1. Preheat the oven to 190°C.
2. Place the almonds on a baking tray and lightly toast them in the oven for 5–8 minutes, until golden brown.
3. Roughly chop the almonds, garlic and basil. Place in a pestle and mortar, add the olive oil and pound to form a smooth paste. Add the tomatoes, sugar and salt and pepper to taste and blend gently.
4. This will keep for about 1 week in the fridge.

✳ All pesto will keep in your fridge for about 1 week, but remember to pour a layer of extra virgin olive oil over the top of the pesto to prevent the basil from going black.

Rocket and Pistachio Pesto

Pesto di rucola e pistacchi

Makes 200ml

Pistachio might seem like an unusual ingredient to add to rocket and Parmesan, but it's delicious. As with all pesto, it's a handy recipe for a quick supper.

150ml extra virgin olive oil
75g unsalted pistachio nuts, shelled
2 garlic cloves
75g rocket
50g freshly grated Parmesan
salt and freshly ground black pepper

1. Roughly chop the nuts, garlic and rocket.
2. Blend all the ingredients in a pestle and mortar to form a smooth paste and check for seasoning. If the sauce seems too thick, loosen it with more extra virgin olive oil.
3. This will keep for about 1 week in the fridge.

✳ Not only can this be served with pasta, but it's also
   delicious with baked fish. Alternatively, add a little more
   olive oil to this pesto and use it as a dip for breads.

Walnut Pesto

Pesto di noci

Makes 200ml

I usually spread this on piadina *(p. 52) and add goat's cheese and rocket for a very tasty lunch.*

75g walnut halves
150ml extra virgin olive oil
2 garlic cloves
40g basil leaves
50g freshly grated Parmesan
salt and freshly ground black pepper

1. Preheat the oven to 190°C.
2. Place the walnuts on a baking tray and toast them in the oven for about 5 minutes. Remove from the oven and rub gently in a dry tea towel to flake the skin off.
3. Roughly chop the walnuts, garlic and basil.
4. Blend all the ingredients in a pestle and mortar to form a smooth paste. Check for seasoning.
5. This will keep for about 1 week in the fridge.

✳ It's quite difficult to remove all the skin from the walnuts, but removing some is better than none, otherwise the pesto can taste a little bitter.

Sage and Lemon Butter

Burro alla salvia e limone

Makes 120ml

A simple sauce, sage and lemon butter is deliciously zingy when drizzled over fish or chicken and especially with ravioli, like the butternut squash ravioli on p. 104.

100g unsalted butter
1 ½ tbsp chopped sage leaves
1 tbsp lemon juice
salt and freshly ground black pepper

1. Melt the butter in a large frying pan until foaming, taking care not to burn the butter. Add the sage and fry for a few seconds. Quickly remove the pan from the heat and add the lemon juice and some salt and pepper to taste.
2. This will keep for about 1 week in the fridge.

* I freeze leftovers in a plastic container. I then simply spoon out individual portions as I need them.

Fish

Roasted Monkfish with Trapanese Pesto
Rana pescatrice arrosto con pesto Trapanese

Seafood Skewers with Lemon, Almond and Rocket Couscous
Spiedini di pesce al limone, con cuscusalle mandorle e rucola

Tuna Steaks with Orange, Spinach and Pine Nut Salad
Bistecche di tonno con insalata di arance, spinaci e pinoli

Char-grilled Squid with Chillies and Aubergines
Calamari picanti e melanzane alla griglia

Sea Bass with Fennel and Garlic
Branzino con finocchio e aglio

Fritto Misto

Livorno-style Fish Stew
Cacciucco

Pistachio-crusted Fillet of Cod with a Shallot, Lemon and Crème Fraîche Sauce
Filetto di merluzzo in crosta di pistacchi con crema allo scalogno e limone

Lemon and Herb-crusted Mussels
Cozze gratinate al limone e erbe aromatiche

Grilled Prawns
Gamberoni alla griglia

Roasted Monkfish with Trapanese Pesto

Rana pescatrice arrosto con pesto Trapanese

Serves 6

If ever there was an impressive one-pot wonder, I think this has to be it! The colours and flavours of the Mediterranean are all here on one roasting tray, so select a nice roasting dish and bring it straight to the table for your well-deserved round of applause from your guests.

extra virgin olive oil

4 red peppers

1kg monkfish tail

4 tbsp Trapanese pesto (p. 133)

salt and freshly ground black pepper

2 red onions, cut into wedges

3 courgettes, cut into 3cm diagonal slices

2 yellow peppers, deseeded and sliced

3 sprigs of rosemary

100g cherry tomatoes on the vine

crusty bread, to serve

1. Preheat the oven to 180°C.
2. Rub some oil over 2 of the red peppers and place them on a baking tray. Roast in the oven for about 30 minutes, until the peppers are fully softened and the skin has browned well. Remove the peppers and place them in a plastic bag or a bowl covered

with cling film. Seal the bag or cover the bowl and leave for about 20 minutes, then remove the peppers and peel off the skin. (By placing the peppers in the bag or the covered bowl, the steam helps loosen the skin, making them much easier to peel.) Discard the skin and the seeds, then quarter the peppers. Set aside.

3. Remove any skin or membrane from the monkfish. Using a sharp knife, cut along one side of the central bone as close to the bone as possible and remove the fish fillet. Repeat on the other side.

4. Lay one fillet out flat, cut side up, and place half the roasted red peppers on top, followed by the pesto and the final layer of roasted red peppers. Place the remaining fish fillet on top, cut side down and head to tail, so that it resembles a sandwich and is an even depth all across the fish. Tie the fish with kitchen string at intervals. Sprinkle with salt and pepper and set aside.

5. Deseed the remaining 2 red peppers and cut into chunks. Add all the vegetables and rosemary to a roasting dish. Drizzle with olive oil and season well. Place the fish on top of the vegetables and place the tomatoes on the top of the fish.

6. Place in the oven for about 45 minutes, or until the fish is cooked through and turns opaque. (It may be necessary to cover the fish with foil if it's browning too much.)

7. To serve, cut the fish into thick slices, remove the string and serve on the roasted vegetables with some crusty bread on the side.

✳ I have also made this dish with fillets of sea bass. In this instance, start the vegetables in the oven first, as the sea bass will cook through in 20 minutes. You could also try cod.

Seafood Skewers with Lemon, Almond and Rocket Couscous

Spiedini di pesce al limone, con cuscusalle mandorle e rucola

Serves 4

Inspired by Fatia el Iba, chef and proprietor of Ey Zemen restaurant in Mazarra, Sicily, who showed me how she prepares her Tunisian–Sicilian couscous dish, I came up with this one. I use the quick-cooking couscous, which is readily available in all supermarkets. Alternatively, you can buy the larger grained couscous and steam it for about 30 minutes. This particular recipe also looks impressive, especially on the BBQ in the summer.

for the seafood skewers:
8 large king prawns
8 squid tubes
400g firm white fish fillets, e.g. monkfish
½ tsp fennel seeds
½ tsp green peppercorns
2 small garlic cloves, finely crushed
1 red chilli, minced
5 tbsp extra virgin olive oil
2 lemons, cut into wedges
8 small bay leaves
salt and freshly ground black pepper

for the couscous:
2 lemons, sliced
3 tbsp extra virgin olive oil
1 garlic clove, finely chopped
1 red chilli, finely chopped
50ml lemon juice
350ml vegetable stock
350g couscous
½ bunch flat-leaf parsley, roughly chopped
40g almond flakes, toasted
salt and freshly ground black pepper
1 large bunch rocket

1. First, soak the skewers if you're using wooden ones.
2. Shell and devein the prawns, leaving the tails on. Cut the squid down the side and then cut across into 1 ½cm slices. Place all the fish in a bowl.
3. Crush the fennel seeds and peppercorns in a pestle and mortar, then add to the fish. Add the garlic, chilli and oil to the fish and allow to marinate for about 15 minutes.
4. Meanwhile, start the couscous. In a dry frying pan, lightly brown the lemon slices. Set aside.
5. Heat the olive oil in another pan. Add the garlic, chilli and lemon juice and cook on a low heat for 2–3 minutes, until the garlic has softened and is slightly golden. Set aside.

6. Bring the stock to the boil, then remove from the heat and add the couscous. Allow to stand for 5 minutes, or until the liquid has been absorbed. Fluff with a fork, then add the garlic/oil mixture to the couscous.
7. Chop the caramelised lemon slices and add them to the couscous. Add the chopped parsley and toasted almonds and check for seasoning. Set aside.
8. Thread the fish onto the soaked skewers with a lemon wedge and a bay leaf in the centre. Season with salt and pepper.
9. Place on a hot grill pan or BBQ for about 2–3 minutes, until the fish is cooked, and turn over and cook for another 2 minutes on the other side. Remove from the heat and set aside.
10. To serve, tear the rocket leaves into the couscous and spoon onto a presentation platter. Place the seafood skewers on top.

* The leftover couscous is delicious as a salad the following day – just add some crumbled feta.

Tuna Steaks with Orange, Spinach and Pine Nut Salad

Bistecche di tonno con insalata di arance, spinaci e pinoli

Serves 4

Sicilian tuna is truly outstanding. Unfortunately, it's in short supply, as most of it is exported to Japan for sushi and sashimi. A strong-flavoured fish, tuna is particularly delicate to cook and can overcook in seconds. It should be pink in the centre to enjoy it at its best.

The olive oil, lemon and garlic sauce that's brushed onto the tuna is typical Sicilian and is called a salmoriglio. *It works well with all fish and meats.*

for the tuna:
1 tbsp lemon juice
100ml extra virgin olive oil
2 garlic cloves, minced
½ tsp dried oregano
salt and freshly ground black pepper
4 x 200g tuna steaks

for the salad:
1 tbsp butter
150g pine nuts
1 ¼ tsp salt, divided
1 tbsp white wine vinegar
½ tsp freshly ground black pepper
1 tbsp honey
100ml extra virgin olive oil
250g baby spinach, washed, drained well and dried
1 small red onion, very thinly sliced
3 oranges, peeled and cut into ½cm slices

1. To make the salad, melt the butter in a heavy-based frying pan and add the pine nuts. Toast the pine nuts over a low to medium heat, stirring constantly and taking care not to burn them, about 2–3 minutes. Sprinkle with ¼ tsp salt and set aside.
2. Using a food processor, add the vinegar, 1 tsp salt, the pepper and honey. With the processor running, slowly drizzle in the oil. Add 2 tbsp of the toasted pine nuts and process to a purée.
3. Place the spinach into a large salad bowl. Add the onion and toss with enough dressing to coat. Taste and add more salt if needed.
4. Arrange the orange slices overlapping around the outer edge of a large, cold serving platter and drizzle with any remaining dressing. Pile the spinach in the centre and sprinkle with the remaining toasted pine nuts. Set aside.

5. To make the sauce for the tuna, add the lemon juice to a bowl and add the oil in a slow, steady stream, whisking vigorously. Finish with the minced garlic, oregano and seasoning. Brush the sauce over the tuna.
6. Heat a griddle pan. Place the tuna in the pan and cook for about 2 minutes on each side. Serve on a bed of the spinach and orange salad.

* I have to thank Franco, Claudio's cousin, for this tip: he lovingly brushes the sauce onto each piece of fish with a sprig of rosemary. The subtle flavour of rosemary that ensues is really worth it.

Char-grilled Squid with Chillies and Aubergines

Calamari picanti e melanzane alla griglia

Serves 4

It's important to choose the right squid for this recipe, definitely no larger than 15cm long, excluding tentacles. The larger ones are better for stews, as they tend to be less tender. The marinade in this recipe is useful for most fish and even for chicken or pork for the BBQ.

2 garlic cloves, chopped
2 small red chillies, deseeded and chopped
4 tbsp extra virgin olive oil
juice of 1 lemon
1 tsp hot chilli sauce
2 squid pouches
2 medium aubergines, thinly sliced
salt and freshly ground black pepper
extra virgin olive oil, for frying
rocket leaves, to serve
lemon wedges, to serve

1. Mix the garlic, chillies, olive oil, lemon juice and chilli sauce in a shallow dish. Slice the squid into rings and add to marinade, stirring well. Cover and refrigerate and leave to marinate for 30 minutes.
2. Meanwhile, degorge the aubergine by placing the slices in a colander and sprinkling with salt. Leave for 30 minutes to allow the bitter juices to drain, then rinse the aubergine and pat dry.
3. Heat a griddle pan (or frying pan) until smoking and brush with oil (alternatively, preheat the grill to high and brush the aubergine slices with oil). Cook the aubergine slices in batches until golden on each side. Keep warm in a low oven.
4. Remove the squid from the marinade using a slotted spoon, reserving the marinade. Heat the frying pan once more and cook (or grill) the squid for 15 seconds on each side. Transfer the squid to a warmed dish and keep hot. Wipe out the pan, pour the marinade in and heat gently.

5. To serve, scatter some rocket leaves on a plate. Create a tower effect by placing an aubergine slice on the rocket. Place a ring of squid on top and another aubergine slice on top of the squid and continue to layer, finishing with the squid. Spoon over a little marinade and serve immediately with lemon wedges.

✳ Marinate for a maximum of 30 minutes, otherwise the lemon will start to cook the squid.

Sea Bass with Fennel and Garlic

Branzino con finocchio e aglio

Serves 4

Sea bass is a delicious, delicate fish that takes simple flavours well. The lemon and anise flavour of the fennel is a great balance for the sweetness of the sea bass. This dish was inspired by an amazing sea bass served at the Monte San Giuliano restaurant in the breathtaking mountaintop village of Erice in Sicily.

4 fennel bulbs, with a few fennel fronds
   reserved for garnish
extra virgin olive oil
4 garlic cloves, halved lengthways
4 tbsp hot water

salt and freshly ground black pepper
2 lemons
20g black olives, halved
4 x 120g sea bass fillets
2 tbsp chopped basil

1. Remove the tough outer layers of the fennel. Chop the fronds and set them aside. Cut the bulbs in half from top to bottom, then cut into 4 wedges.
2. Heat about 3 tbsp olive oil in a heavy-based pan. Add the fennel and fry over a high heat, stirring from time to time, until it begins to turn golden brown. Add the garlic and cook for 1 minute. Add the hot water and season with salt and pepper.
3. Cover the pan, turn the heat down and cook for about 10 minutes, until the fennel is tender and all the liquid has been absorbed.
4. Meanwhile, juice one of the lemons and mix it with 100ml olive oil. Season with salt and pepper. Quarter the other lemon and set aside.
5. When the fennel is done, add the olives and remove the pan from the heat. Add the fennel fronds and drizzle with a little olive oil. Set aside and keep warm.
6. Slash 1cm-deep cuts across the skin of the fish fillets and season with the chopped basil, pushing it into the slashes.
7. Preheat a frying pan. Brush the fish with olive oil and place in the pan. Cook for about 2 minutes. Turn over and sauté for another 3 minutes, or until cooked through.
8. To serve, place the grilled fish on serving plates, pour the lemon and oil dressing over and scatter with any remaining basil. Add a wedge of lemon to each portion. Serve with the fennel and olives on the side.

* When sautéing fish, place the presentation side first into the pan. This ensures that the 'good' side isn't too brown from the caramelised cooking juices in the pan.

Fritto Misto

Serves 4

I prefer this recipe for fritto misto, as it gives a clean, crispy coating and avoids the mess that usually results from an egg batter. The mix of frutti di mare (the seafood) and the seasonal vegetables makes a wonderful fresh combination for the fritto misto platter.

200g monkfish, cut into 2cm cubes
175g whole small prawns
175g squid, cut into rings
2 fillets of any firm white fish, e.g. monkfish, cut into squares
200g Italian '00' flour or strong white flour
1 tsp cayenne pepper
salt and freshly ground black pepper
olive oil or sunflower oil, for frying
1 courgette, thinly sliced
1 fennel bulb, thinly sliced
sparkling water
lemon wedges, to serve

1. Chill all the fish together over a bowl of ice.
2. Mix the flour and cayenne together, adding some salt and pepper to season.
3. Heat the oil in a deep fryer to 180°C.
4. Dip the fish in the flour, shaking off the excess, then place into the heated oil and fry for 2–3 minutes, taking care not to overload the pan. Remove with a slotted spoon and drain on kitchen paper. Continue until all the fish is cooked and keep warm in a low oven.
5. To prepare the vegetables, first dip them in sparkling water and then in the flour and immediately cook in the hot oil.
6. To serve, toss the fish and vegetables together and sprinkle with salt and pepper. Place on a wooden platter and serve with lemon wedges.

✳ To see if the oil is sufficiently hot for deep frying, test it first with a cube of bread. Alternatively, place the handle of a wooden spoon in the hot oil. When the oil is sufficiently hot, it will cause the moisture in the handle to rise. Allow the oil to return to 180°C between batches of frying.

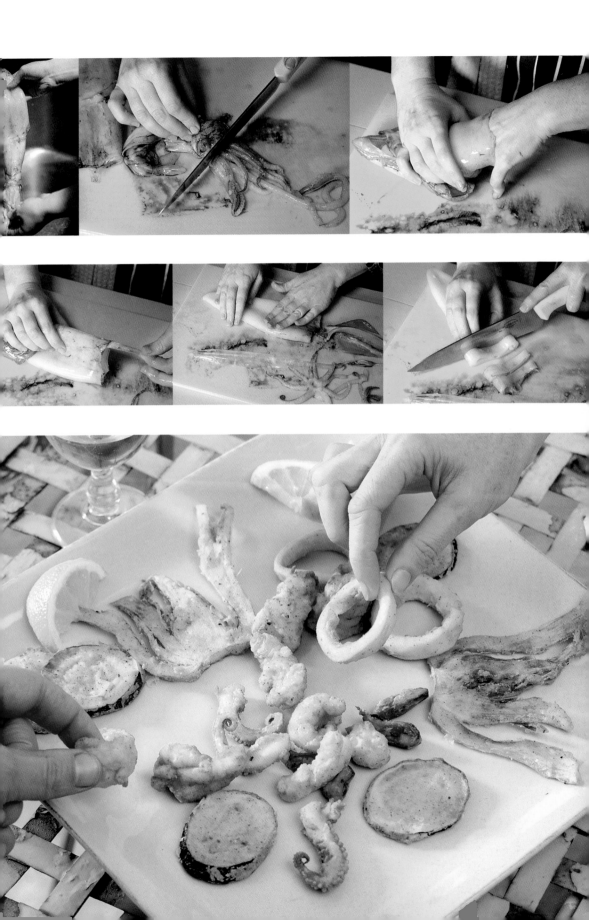

Livorno-style Fish Stew

Cacciucco

Serves 4

Fish soups and stews were originally a fisherman's staple and were meant to use up all the fish that didn't sell. These days, such dishes have become specialities. As traditional and local ingredients are still used, such stews will vary from region to region. For example, a Sicilian stew will usually have todari *and* polpo, *a large squid and octopus. Cacciucco means 'mixture of seafood' and is originally from Livorno. Garlic is essential in this dish.*

450g mussels

300g clams

200g prawns

500g red snapper or sea bass (Pollock or Gurnard)

extra virgin olive oil

1 carrot, finely diced

1 ½ celery stalks, finely sliced

4 garlic cloves, chopped

½ x 400g tin of cherry tomatoes

pinch of saffron

½ red chilli, chopped

3 sprigs of thyme

350ml red wine

500ml fish stock

salt and freshly ground black pepper

1 small bunch of parsley, chopped

crusty bread, to serve

1. Trim the beards from the mussels and rinse along with the clams in cold water. Drain well. Throw out any shellfish that won't close when tapped. Shell the prawns and cut the snapper or sea bass into bite-sized pieces. Set aside.
2. Heat some olive oil in a large saucepan. Add the carrot and celery and sauté for 5 minutes. Add the garlic and sauté for 1 minute more. Add the cherry tomatoes, saffron, chilli and thyme and stir. Add the wine, stock and the snapper or sea bass and simmer for 8–10 minutes. Finally, add the mussels, clams and prawns and simmer for 5 minutes.
3. Remove the thyme sprigs. Discard any mussels or clams that have not opened. Taste for seasoning. Sprinkle with the parsley and serve with crusty bread.

✳ The red wine can be replaced with white wine in this recipe for a more subtle flavour.

Pistachio-crusted Fillet of Cod with Shallot, Lemon and Crème Fraîche Sauce

Filetto di merluzzo in crosta di pistacchi con crema allo scalogno e limone

Serves 4

This recipe came about from a wonderful antipasto that I had in Rome, a tail of red mullet with pistachio. Sometimes I replace the pistachio with macadamia nuts, yum!

for the pistachio-crusted cod:
flour, for dredging
salt and freshly ground black pepper
2 egg whites, lightly beaten
1 tbsp milk
250g pistachio nuts, chopped medium-fine
4 cod fillets
extra virgin olive oil
lemon wedges, to garnish

for the lemon and crème fraîche sauce:
extra virgin olive oil
2 small shallots (or 1 medium), finely chopped
120ml fish stock
zest of 1 lemon
3 tbsp crème fraîche
1 tbsp finely chopped flat-leaf parsley
salt and freshly ground black pepper

1. To prepare the cod, place the flour in a wide, shallow bowl and season it well with salt and pepper. Beat the egg whites and milk together in a second wide, shallow bowl. Place the nuts in a third wide, shallow bowl.
2. Dust each fillet lightly with the seasoned flour. Dip the fish into the egg white mix, then coat with chopped nuts. Allow the fish to rest in the fridge for 30–60 minutes.
3. Heat the oil in a frying pan over a moderate heat. Sauté the fish for 3–4 minutes per side, until crisp and firm to the touch. Set aside and keep warm.
4. For the sauce, heat a little olive oil in a frying pan. Sauté the shallots on a low heat for 3–4 minutes, until soft. Add the stock and lemon zest and simmer for 3–4 minutes. Stir in the crème fraîche and parsley, then heat through. Season to taste.
5. Place the cod fillets on serving plates and pour the sauce over. Garnish with a lemon wedge.

✳ For a smoother sauce, whizz in a blender.

156

Lemon and Herb-crusted Mussels

Cozze gratinate al limone e erbe aromatiche

Serves 4

I also really like to make this recipe with clams, which are sweet when grilled. And it's such an easy starter – it only takes minutes to make. Not only that, it's also very impressive for entertaining or served as canapés with drinks.

2kg mussels
80ml boiling water
100g butter
2 tsp olive oil
2 garlic cloves

2 shallots, roughly chopped
4 tbsp chopped parsley, plus extra to garnish
zest and juice of 1 lemon
salt and freshly ground black pepper
120g fresh breadcrumbs

1. Trim the beards from the mussels and rinse in cold water. Drain well. Throw out any mussels that won't close when tapped.
2. Place the mussels in a large saucepan with the boiling water. Cover and cook for 4 minutes, or until the mussels have opened. Drain in a colander and discard any mussels that have not opened. Set aside.
3. Preheat the grill.
4. Place the butter, olive oil, garlic, shallots, parsley, lemon zest and salt and pepper in a blender or food processor and blitz to a coarse texture.
5. Remove the top half of the mussel shell and discard, keeping only the shell halves that contain the mussels. Arrange them on a baking tray. Spoon a little of the butter mixture on each mussel and sprinkle with breadcrumbs.
6. Grill for about 3 minutes, until golden. Sprinkle with the lemon juice and extra parsley and serve.

✳ Save the cooking liquid from the mussels for a fish stock for your chowder or to make a sauce to accompany fish. I usually freeze it until needed.

✳ This dish can also be prepared in advance to just before the grilling point. Keep the mussels refrigerated until needed.

157

Grilled Prawns

Gamberoni alla griglia

Serves 4–6

Dublin Bay prawns are the best in the world. They are best prepared as simply as possible to showcase their wonderfully sweet flavour and delicious meaty texture. When we're in Sicily, we leave the prawns whole for this recipe and grill them over hot coals. The scent of the prawns grilling always guarantees to gather the clan quickly.

for the prawns:
12–16 Dublin Bay prawns
½ tsp salt
½ tsp freshly ground black pepper
zest of ½ lemon
1 tsp chopped parsley

for the dressing:
6 tbsp extra virgin olive oil
2 garlic cloves, chopped
juice of 1 lemon

1. Preheat the grill.
2. Using a sharp knife, slice the prawns in half lengthways. Remove the black vein and discard.
3. Mix the salt, pepper, lemon zest and parsley together.
4. Place the prawns on a grilling tray and sprinkle the seasoned salt mixture over. Grill the prawns, flesh side up, for about 4–5 minutes.
5. Meanwhile, heat the oil and gently sauté the garlic for about 2 minutes, taking care not to let it burn. Allow to cool and add the lemon juice, mixing well.
6. When the prawns are ready and still piping hot, drizzle the dressing over and serve immediately.

✳ Baste the prawns with thyme sprigs dipped into the dressing or even add rosemary or thyme to your coals in the BBQ.

Poultry, Meat and Game

Roast Lemon Chicken with Fennel and Lemon Risotto Stuffing
Pollo arrosto ripieno di risotto al limone e finocchio

Hunter's Chicken
Pollo al cacciatore

Palermo-style Steak
Bistecca alla Palermitana

Pizza Makers' Wives' Steak
Bistecca all pizzaiola

Braised Beef with Garlic, Lemon and Chilli
Brasato di manzo all'aglio, limone e peperoncino

Roman Chianino Beef Fillet with a Chestnut Mushroom
and Chianti Sauce
Filetto di manzo con salsa al Chianti e funghi

Meatballs in Spicy Tomato Sauce
Polpette di carne in salsa di pomodoro piccante

Ossobuco alla Milanese with Saffron Risotto
Ossobuco alla milanese con risotto allo zafferano

Roasted Pork Belly with Lemon, Honey and Thyme
Arrosto di pancia di maiale con limone, miele e timo

Escalopes of Pork with Sage and Prosciutto
Saltimbocca alla Romana

Pork with Orange Marsala Sauce
Maiale con salsa di arancia e Marsala

Butterflied Leg of Lamb with Lemon Dressing
Cosciotto di agnello al limone

Braised Shoulder of Lamb in a Red Wine and Bean Sauce
Brasato di spalla d'agnello con salsa ai cannelloni e vino rosso

Braised Rabbit with Marsala and Sage Sauce
Brasato di coniglio con salsa di Marsala e salvia

Roast Pheasant with Pancetta, White Wine and Rosemary
Arrosto di fagiano con pancetta, vino bianco e rosmarino

Roast Lemon Chicken with Fennel and Lemon Risotto Stuffing

Pollo arrosto ripieno di risotto al limone e finocchio

Serves 6

This is a very tasty and unusual stuffing. The proportion of liquid to rice for the risotto is lower than normal, but the risotto cooks in the chicken and absorbs some of the chicken juices at the same time. I sometimes prepare the risotto for supper (adding more stock) and use the leftovers the following day to stuff a chicken breast, which I oven bake.

2 large sprigs of thyme
75g butter, softened
salt and freshly ground black pepper
1 x 1 ½kg chicken, free-range and
   organic if possible
6 slices pancetta (or smoked streaky bacon)
extra virgin olive oil

1 fennel bulb, finely diced
100g Arborio rice
zest of 1 lemon
juice of ½ lemon
120ml white wine
100ml chicken stock
baked fennel with lemon and olives
   (p. 194), to serve

1. Preheat the oven to 190°C.
2. Remove the leaves from one of the thyme sprigs. Mix with the softened butter and season with salt and pepper. Spread the herb butter over the chicken and place the pancetta (or streaky bacon) on top.
3. Heat some olive oil in a saucepan. Fry the fennel and the remaining whole sprig of thyme gently for 5–7 minutes, until the fennel has softened. Add the rice and lemon zest, mixing well.
4. Add the lemon juice and white wine and simmer until the wine has soaked into the rice. Add the stock. Bring to the boil and simmer, stirring all the time, for about 4–5 minutes, or until the stock has been absorbed by the rice. Remove the thyme sprig and discard.
5. Remove the rice from the heat and spoon it into the chicken cavity, taking care not to pack it too tightly. Tie the chicken legs gently together to keep in the stuffing. Weigh the stuffed bird. Calculate the cooking time based on 20 minutes per 500g, plus an additional 20 minutes.

6. Roast the chicken for approximately 1 ½ – 2 hours, until cooked through, basting from time to time. Check the chicken is done by inserting a skewer into the thickest part of the leg. If the juices run clear, the chicken is cooked. Remove the chicken from the oven, cover with foil and rest for 15 minutes before serving. Serve with the baked fennel (p. 194).

* Add some dried apricots or chestnuts and a sprig of rosemary to the stuffing. For an even more delicious result, replace the thyme with lemon thyme.

Hunter's Chicken

Pollo al cacciatore

Serves 6

This is a classic that will never let you down. This recipe works well with pheasant or rabbit too. If using diced chicken breast rather than thigh, do take care not to overcook it, as the chicken dries out and becomes stringy in texture. And it's always best to add olives as the last ingredient to a dish, as they can become quite bitter if overcooked.

1.5kg whole chicken, segmented
2 tbsp plain flour, seasoned with salt and
   freshly ground black pepper
extra virgin olive oil
1 large onion, finely chopped
2 garlic cloves, finely chopped
2 x 400g tins of tomatoes
500ml chicken stock

125ml white wine
2 tbsp tomato purée
1 tsp caster sugar
2 tbsp chopped basil
2 tbsp chopped parsley
90g black olives, stoned and quartered
boiled rice or tagliatelle, to serve

1. Toss the chicken segments in the seasoned flour, shaking off the excess flour.
2. Heat some olive oil in a frying pan. Brown the chicken pieces in batches over a medium heat (take care not to overcrowd the frying pan). Remove the chicken from the pan and place in a separate saucepan or casserole dish.
3. Cook the onions in the frying pan over a low heat for 7–10 minutes, until soft. Add the garlic and cook gently for 1 minute more. Add the tomatoes, stock and wine. Bring to the boil, reduce the heat and simmer for 15 minutes. Add the tomato purée and sugar and stir.
4. Pour the sauce over the chicken and stir well. Cover and simmer for 30 minutes, then add the herbs and olives. Season with salt and pepper to taste and serve.

* Glam it up by adding 125g sautéed mushrooms, or green peppers and capers for an extra bite.

Palermo-style Steak

Bistecca alla Palermitana

Serves 4

This is a lovely twist on a simple steak. Not only does it look good, but it's also packed with flavour. I first tried this steak in a little side street trattoria in Palermo and couldn't wait to make it for the family as soon as I got home to Wicklow. My dad, a true Irish farmer, is passionate about meat and gave this recipe two thumbs up.

Sometimes I add a few chilli flakes to the breadcrumbs or even ¼ tsp of paprika.

4 sirloin steaks
2 tbsp plain flour
1 egg, beaten
150g breadcrumbs
4 tbsp freshly grated Parmesan
2 garlic cloves, crushed
2 tsp finely chopped parsley

zest of 1 lemon
salt and freshly ground black pepper
extra virgin olive oil
lemon wedges, to serve
garlic and sage roast potatoes (p. 192), to serve
green salad, to serve

1. Tenderise the steaks by flattening them until they're 1 ½cm thick between 2 sheets of cling film using a meat tenderiser.
2. Place the flour on one plate and the beaten egg on a second plate. Mix the breadcrumbs, Parmesan, garlic, parsley, lemon zest and salt and pepper together on a third plate.
3. Dip the steak into the flour and shake off the excess, then brush both sides of the steak lightly with the beaten egg. Coat the steak in the breadcrumb mixture.
4. Heat some olive oil in a large frying pan. Cook the steak over a high heat to sear both sides, then reduce the heat to medium and continue cooking for anything from 1–4 minutes, depending how well done you like your steak.
5. Place on a warm plate and serve with lemon wedges, garlic and sage roast potatoes (p. 192) and a green salad.

✱ Use a rolling pin to tenderise the meat if you don't have a meat tenderiser. Also, if garlic tends to burn in your pan, then replace the fresh garlic with garlic powder.

Pizza Makers' Wives' Steak

Bistecca all pizzaiola

Serves 4

Originally from Naples, nowadays you'll see this dish all over Italy. This was one of the first dishes that my husband Claudio made for me. The sauce is also delicious served with sirloin steaks that have been tenderised with a meat tenderiser (see p. 165) and flash fried.

4 T-bone steaks
salt and freshly ground black pepper
3 tbsp extra virgin olive oil
4 garlic cloves, chopped
¼ tsp chilli flakes
4 small sprigs oregano, chopped, or 1 tsp dried oregano
250ml white wine
350ml tomato sauce (p. 130)
potato and tomato bake (p. 191), to serve

1. Season the steaks with salt and pepper.
2. Heat some oil in a large frying pan. Add the garlic and sauté for 1 minute. Remove the garlic with a slotted spoon and set aside. Add the steak to the pan and quickly brown on each side. Transfer to a warm platter.
3. Add the sautéed garlic, chilli flakes, oregano and wine to the pan. Keep stirring and allow the liquid to reduce slightly. Add the tomato sauce, followed by the steaks. Reduce the heat and cook for 4–9 minutes, depending on how well done you like the steaks. Add a little water if the sauce is too thick.
4. Transfer the steaks to a serving platter, pour over the sauce and serve immediately with the potato and tomato bake (p. 191).

* Add some capers and green olives at the end for a new dimension to the sauce.

Braised Beef with Garlic, Lemon and Chilli

Brasato di manzo all'aglio, limone e peperoncino

Serves 4–5

A good beef stew is always a winner, and this recipe has an added interest in the form of a buttato (meaning 'a throw'), which is additional chopped ingredients added in at the end of a dish to further enliven the taste buds. I like to make this dish for entertaining and leave the buttato in the centre of the table for guests to add to their plates themselves.

The idea for a buttato was given to me by chef Marino Monterisi, who along with his business partner, Alvaro Herran, runs the ever-popular Irish–Italian restaurant, Bates, in our local town of Rathdrum.

extra virgin olive oil

4 onions, chopped

1kg round steak, trimmed and cut into cubes

1 ½ tbsp flour seasoned with salt and pepper

350ml medium-bodied red wine

1 x 400g tin of chopped tomatoes

2 bay leaves

salt and freshly ground black pepper

1 tsp sugar

sautéed broccoli (p. 198), to serve

for the buttato:

2 garlic cloves, finely chopped

1 large red chilli (or to taste), finely chopped

zest of 1 lemon

1. Heat some oil in a large saucepan. Fry the onions on a low heat for 7–10 minutes, until soft.
2. Meanwhile, toss the beef in the seasoned flour. Heat some oil in a separate frying pan and brown the meat, taking care not to overcrowd the pan, as the meat will stew rather than brown. Add the meat to the saucepan containing the onions. Deglaze the frying pan with a good splash of the red wine. Pour these juices over the meat and onions and mix in the remaining red wine. Bring to a boil, then reduce to a simmer for about 10 minutes.

3. Add in the chopped tomatoes along with the bay leaves, salt, pepper and sugar. Bring the sauce back to the boil, cover with a lid and allow to simmer gently for about 2 hours, until the meat is nice and tender. Stir the meat occasionally to check that it's not sticking to the bottom of the pan and add in a little hot water if needed.
4. When the beef is ready, add in the *buttato* seasonings. Add salt and pepper to taste and serve with sautéed broccoli (p. 198).

* Adjust the buttato to your taste. You could replace the lemon with orange zest or add some sun-dried tomatoes or chopped parsley.

Roman Chianina Beef Fillet with a Chestnut Mushroom and Chianti Sauce

Filetto di manzo con salsa al Chianti e funghi

Serves 4

Dating from ancient Roman times, Chianina cattle are a large, stocky breed, white or sometimes grey in colour, and are raised in the Val di Chiana, near Arezzo. This rich Chianti sauce works well with any cut of beef or game.

4 x 180g beef fillets
salt and freshly ground black pepper
extra virgin olive oil
2 shallots, cut into wedges
150g chestnut mushrooms, sliced

1 tsp chopped thyme
250ml Chianti
1 tbsp tomato purée
2 tsp butter

1. Season the beef fillets with salt and pepper. Heat some olive oil in a frying pan. Add the fillets and cook both sides over a high heat for 2–3 minutes or longer, depending on how well done you like your steak. Transfer the fillets to a platter to rest and keep warm in a low oven.
2. Add the shallots to the pan and sauté over a low heat for 5 minutes. Add in the mushrooms and thyme, increasing the heat and stirring constantly for another 5 minutes, until the mushrooms are cooked (see also the tip on cooking mushrooms on p. 88).
3. Add the wine and the tomato purée. Allow the sauce to thicken slightly and add the butter. Remove from the heat immediately and season with salt and pepper.
4. Pour the sauce over the fillets and garnish with a sprig of thyme. Serve immediately.

✳ Try the same sauce with lamb chops and replace the thyme with rosemary.

Meatballs in Spicy Tomato Sauce

Polpette di carne in salsa di pomodoro piccante

Serves 6 Ⓔ Ⓕ

Meatballs form the secondi *or meat course at the Italian table, while pasta is the* primi, *so they would not traditionally be served together. That said, they work well together, so if this takes your fancy, allow 400–450g dried spaghetti to serve four. I also sometimes add 50g freshly grated Parmesan to the meatballs and reduce the salt, yum!*

for the meatballs:
50g fresh breadcrumbs
100ml milk
1 onion, finely chopped
1 garlic clove, finely chopped
225g minced pork
225g lean minced beef
1 tsp dried oregano
1 tsp salt
½ tsp freshly ground black pepper
1 egg, beaten
extra virgin olive oil

for the spicy tomato sauce:
1 tbsp extra virgin olive oil
1 red chilli, deseeded and finely chopped
1 onion, finely chopped
2 cloves garlic, finely chopped
175ml vegetable stock
500g tinned chopped tomatoes
2 tbsp tomato purée
salt and freshly ground black pepper
pasta, to serve
freshly grated Parmesan, to serve

1. To make the meatballs, first soak the breadcrumbs in the milk.
2. Mix the chopped onion and garlic with the pork and beef. Add the breadcrumbs, oregano, salt and pepper to the meat mixture and mix well. Add in the beaten egg and mix thoroughly. Roll the mixture into small balls.
3. Heat some oil in a frying pan and add in the meatballs. Fry for approximately 5 minutes, turning occasionally, until browned on all sides. Remove from the heat and set aside.
4. To make the sauce, heat the oil in a large saucepan. Add the chilli and onion and cook on a low heat for 7–10 minutes, until softened. Add the garlic, stock, tinned tomatoes, tomato purée, salt and pepper. Bring to the boil and allow to simmer for 5 minutes. Add the meatballs to the sauce and leave to simmer for 10 minutes to heat through.
5. Serve with your favourite pasta and sprinkle grated Parmesan on top.

* Have a bowl of cold water beside you to dip your hands into. This prevents the meat from sticking when forming the meatballs.

Ossobuco alla Milanese with Saffron Risotto

Ossobuco alla milanese con risotto allo zafferano

Serves 4

The Italian staple! This is certainly a hearty dish. If veal isn't to your liking, I've tried this recipe with pork shank and bone-in pork chops and they were both delicious. I've also made it with chicken legs and thighs, which is lovely but a far cry from the original recipe, considering the veal shank is the ossobuco. One thing is for sure, though – the gremolata is a must with the recipe, as it gives the dish its final lift.

Ask your butcher to prepare the veal shank chops for you. They may also need to be tied together to hold in the stew.

for the *ossobuco*:
6 tbsp flour
salt and freshly ground black pepper
4 veal shanks, cut across into chops
    about 5cm thick
extra virgin olive oil
120ml dry white wine
1 x 400g tin of chopped tomatoes
2 tbsp chopped sage
1 tbsp sugar
500ml chicken or beef stock

for the risotto:
1 tbsp extra virgin olive oil
knob of butter
1 onion, finely chopped
1 garlic clove, finely chopped
2–3 saffron threads
400g Arborio rice
150ml white wine
1.2l chicken stock, heated to simmering
50g freshly grated Parmesan
salt and freshly ground black pepper

for the *gremolata*:
1 garlic clove, finely chopped
4 tbsp parsley
1 tbsp lemon zest

1. To make the *ossobuco*, season the flour with salt and pepper, then coat the veal with the flour, shaking off any excess flour.

2. Heat some oil in a heavy casserole dish or a large saucepan. Add the veal to the pan and brown on all sides. This might need to be done in batches, depending on the size of the shank chops. Add the wine and allow to simmer for about 2 minutes. Stir in the tomatoes, sage and sugar. Bring to the boil and simmer, uncovered, for 10 minutes. Add the stock, cover the pot and simmer gently for 1–1 ½ hours, or until the veal is really tender and starts to fall away from the bone. Check the sauce – it should be fairly thick. If not, boil rapidly to reduce. Check for seasoning, adding salt, pepper and sugar as necessary.

3. To make the *gremolata*, mix the garlic with the parsley and lemon zest. Set aside.

4. Meanwhile, to make the risotto, heat the olive oil and butter in a large, heavy-based saucepan. When the butter is foaming, add the onion and cook for 5–7 minutes, until fully softened. Add the garlic, saffron and rice and cook for a few minutes, stirring continuously, until the rice is shiny and opaque. Add the wine and simmer for 1 minute, stirring constantly. Reduce the heat and add the hot stock a ladleful at a time, stirring constantly, until each ladleful is absorbed. The rice should be creamy but firm to the bite. Remove from the heat and stir in the Parmesan. Check for seasoning.

5. To serve, plate the risotto with a veal shank on top and pour over the lovely sauce. Sprinkle the *gremolata* over and serve immediately.

∗ Try this with garlic mashed potatoes or green mash (add some pesto to your mashed potatoes) or Parmesan soft polenta (p. 84) instead of the risotto.

Roasted Pork Belly with Lemon, Honey and Thyme

Arrosto di pancia di maiale con limone, miele e timo

Serves 4

Pork belly has become one of the 'in' meats, as it's so economical and full of flavour.
The glaze is really important to complete this dish. As an alternative, I sometimes mix
some orange juice, powdered ginger and honey for a delicious finish.

1.5kg pork belly (bone in)
sea salt and freshly ground black pepper
1 tbsp fresh thyme
2 onions, halved
2 carrots, cut into chunks
200ml white wine
4 tbsp honey
1 lemon
300ml chicken stock
Fagioli alla Maruzzara (p. 193), to serve

1. Preheat the oven to 150°C.
2. Debone and skin the pork belly. Score diagonal lines across the top side of the pork with a sharp knife. Rub with salt, pepper and the thyme.
3. Place the onions, carrots and the pork bones into the roasting tin. Cover with the removed skin. This is now your trivet onto which you place the pork belly, scored side up. Pour the white wine into the roasting tin.
4. Roast for about 2 hours, until the pork is cooked through. Cover with foil if the scored skin is browning too quickly.
5. Meanwhile, mix the honey and lemon juice together to make the glaze. Set aside.
6. Remove the pork from the oven. Using a pastry brush, glaze the pork by pouring the honey and lemon mix over the top of the pork. Pop the glazed pork belly back in a hot oven (about 200°C) to brown for 10 minutes. Remove the meat from the oven, put it on a plate and cover with aluminium foil to allow it to rest.

7. Deglaze the roasting tin by placing it on the hob, adding the chicken stock and mixing well. Strain the juices from the pan into a saucepan and bring to a simmer to reduce and until it thickens slightly.

8. Serve the pork with *Fagioli alla Maruzzara* (p. 193) and the sauce spooned over.

✳ Ask your butcher to debone and skin the pork, but make sure to keep the bones for the recipe.

Escalopes of Pork with Sage and Prosciutto

Saltimbocca alla Romana

Serves 4

This is one of my favourite Roman dishes. Saltimbocca means 'jump into the mouth'! The pork is beautifully tender in this recipe, but do be careful not to overcook it or it will dry out. This dish also works well with boneless, flattened pork chops or with chicken breast or veal.

4 pork escalopes, about 1cm thick (see tip below)
salt and freshly ground black pepper
12 small sage leaves
8 slices prosciutto
extra virgin olive oil
200ml white wine
40g butter
potato and Parmesan gratin (p. 190), to serve

1. Season the pork with salt and pepper. Place 3 sage leaves on the top side of each piece of pork, then wrap 2 slices of prosciutto around each escalope and fasten underneath with cocktail sticks.
2. Heat some olive oil in a frying pan. Cook the pork over a medium-high heat for 3 minutes on each side, until golden and cooked through. Remove from the pan and keep warm.
3. Pour the white wine into the pan and cook for 4–5 minutes, until the alcohol has cooked off. Melt the butter and remove the pan from the heat.
4. Remove the cocktail sticks from the escalopes and serve with the sauce and potato and Parmesan gratin (p. 190).

✳ To get an even, flat escalope, place the slice of pork fillet between 2 pieces of cling film and flatten out with a rolling pin or mallet.

Pork with Orange Marsala Sauce

Maiale con salsa di arancia e Marsala

Serves 6

This is a typical Sicilian winter dish, when oranges are in season. I first enjoyed this at a family gathering on New Year's Day in Palermo. Marsala is a lovely aperitif and is also very versatile for making sauces. While not the same, sweet sherry can be used as a replacement for the Marsala in this recipe.

3 garlic cloves, finely chopped
zest and juice of 2 oranges
1 red chilli, finely chopped
salt and freshly ground black pepper
extra virgin olive oil
800g boneless loin of pork
2 onions, sliced
3 tbsp Marsala
potato and Parmesan gratin (p. 190), to serve

1. Preheat the oven to 180°C.
2. Mix the garlic, orange zest, chilli, salt and pepper with 2 tbsp olive oil and rub over the pork.
3. On the hob, heat a little oil in an ovenproof frying pan or casserole dish and sear the pork. Add the onions and another drizzle of olive oil. Add the Marsala and 3 tbsp orange juice.
4. Roast for 30–35 minutes, until the pork is cooked through. Remove the pork from the pan and place on a warm platter, covering with foil to rest.
5. Place the pan on the hob. Skim any oil from the cooking juices and simmer for 2–3 minutes. Check for seasoning, adding salt and pepper as required. Add the remainder of the orange juice and stir.
6. Slice the pork, arranging it on a serving platter or individual plates. Place the onions on top and drizzle with the orange sauce. Serve with potato and Parmesan gratin (p. 190).

✳ This also works well if using lemon and rosemary instead of the orange and Marsala. To enrich the sauce, add some fresh cream at the end.

Butterflied Leg of Lamb with Lemon Dressing

Cosciotto di agnello al limone

Serves 6–8

While in the Nebrodi Mountains, our wonderful host, Tullio Scurrio, arranged a mountainside picnic for us. Imagine my delight when we arrived at an old shepherd's mountain hut and outside, there must have been at least 30 local people, from wine producers to cheese makers, from olive farmers to shepherds. And there, grilling on the BBQ, was the most delicious lamb I have ever tasted (aside from Wicklow lamb, of course!). There were local musicians and dancers and the atmosphere was pure magic. So when I make this dish on my BBQ, I close my eyes and dream of the Nebrodi Mountains.

for the leg of lamb:
zest of 1 lemon
juice of 2 lemons
1 tsp crushed fennel seeds
4 tbsp extra virgin olive oil
1.5kg leg of lamb – ask you butcher
    to debone and butterfly it
3 garlic cloves, cut in half lengthways
5 rosemary sprigs
salt and freshly ground black pepper

for the lemon dressing:
170ml extra virgin olive oil
juice of 1 lemon
1 tsp honey
salt and freshly ground black pepper

roasted pumpkin with shallots and orange (p. 197),
    to serve

1. To make the marinade for the lamb, mix the lemon zest and juice, fennel seeds and olive oil and rub it all over the lamb. Pierce the skin at intervals and insert the halved garlic cloves and rosemary sprigs. Place in a covered bowl or large tray and refrigerate overnight.
2. Preheat the oven to 190°C.
3. Bring the lamb to room temperature (allow about 30 minutes for this). Strain the lamb from the marinade and pat it dry. Place a roasting tin on the hob and brown the lamb on all sides. Then place a rack in the roasting tin and put the lamb on top, skin side up. Season with salt and pepper.

4. Roast the lamb for about 1 hour for medium-rare, basting from time to time. Cook for a further 10 minutes if you don't want the lamb too pink. Allow to rest for 10 minutes in a warm place.
5. Meanwhile, to make the dressing, whisk all the ingredients together until emulsified.
6. Transfer the lamb onto a platter and spoon over the lemon dressing to serve. Serve with roasted pumpkin with shallots and orange (p. 197).

*️ Add some mustard or chopped chilli to the dressing for an extra bite.

Braised Shoulder of Lamb in a Red Wine and Bean Sauce

Brasato di spalla d'agnello con salsa ai cannelloni e vino rosso

Serves 6

Lamb is hugely popular in Italy and especially in Rome. This recipe results in melt-in-the-mouth soft, delicious meat. As it has lots of vegetables and beans, it's also quite a light dish.

extra virgin olive oil

1.3kg lamb shoulder, trimmed, boned and tied

3 large garlic cloves, cut into quarters

2 rosemary sprigs, cut to make 12 pieces total

100g smoked pancetta, chopped into 1–1 ½ cm dice

1 onion, finely diced

3 carrots, finely diced

3 celery stalks, finely sliced

1 leek, finely sliced

150ml red wine

300ml lamb stock

1 x 400g tin chopped tomatoes

salt and freshly ground black pepper

3 sprigs of fresh thyme

2 bay leaves

400g cooked cannellini beans, drained and rinsed

1. Heat the oil in a large frying pan and brown the lamb on all sides. Remove from the pan and leave to stand until it's cool enough to handle.
2. When the lamb is cool enough, make 12 deep incisions into the meat. Push a piece of garlic and a small piece of rosemary into each incision.
3. Add the pancetta and onion to the saucepan and sauté for about 5 minutes. Add the carrots, celery and leek to the pan and cook for about 10 minutes, until soft, then transfer to a large casserole cooking pot.
4. Stir the red wine into the cooking pot, then add the stock and chopped tomatoes and season with salt and pepper. Add the thyme sprigs and bay leaves, submerging them in the liquid. Place the lamb on top, cover with the lid and simmer on a low heat for 1 ½ hours, until the lamb is cooked and tender. Using a meat fork or tongs, turn the lamb half way through the cooking time.
5. Remove the lamb from the cooking pot using slotted spoons. Cover the lamb with foil to keep warm and leave to rest for 10 minutes.

6. Stir the beans into the vegetable mixture and warm through.
7. Remove the string from the lamb and carve the meat into thick slices. Remove the thyme sprigs and bay leaves from the vegetable and bean mixture and carefully skim off any fat from the surface. Spoon the vegetables into warmed serving plates and arrange the sliced lamb on top.

* For even more flavour, ask your butcher to stuff the lamb, or bring your own favourite stuffing mix to the butcher for inclusion in the dish.

Braised Rabbit with Marsala and Sage Sauce

Brasato di coniglio con salsa di Marsala e salvia

Serves 4

*Rabbit is frequently cooked at home, most of it caught by the hunters in the family.
The cream and Marsala make a lovely rich sauce that works equally well with chicken,
turkey, pork and game.*

2 rabbits, jointed (ask your butcher to do this)
salt and freshly ground black pepper
extra virgin olive oil
2 onions, thinly sliced
150g wild mushrooms, sliced
3 garlic cloves, chopped

2 tbsp chopped sage
5 slices pancetta, diced
400ml chicken stock
100ml white wine
120ml cream

1. Preheat the oven to 180°C.
2. Season the rabbit pieces with salt and pepper. Heat some olive oil in a frying pan, then
    add the rabbit pieces and brown. Transfer the pieces to an ovenproof casserole dish.
3. Sauté the onions in the same pan on a low heat for 7–10 minutes, then add to the
    rabbit. Next sauté the mushrooms, garlic and sage on a low heat for 4–5 minutes,
    stirring constantly, and add to the casserole. Add the pancetta to the pan and brown
    until it's crispy, then add to the dish.
4. Deglaze the pan with the stock and wine and pour over the other ingredients in the
    casserole. Place in the oven and cook for 40–50 minutes, until the rabbit is tender.
    Remove the meat and stir the cream into the sauce. Serve the rabbit with the sauce
    spooned over.

＊ If a thicker sauce is preferred, simply simmer it to reduce
while keeping the meat warm.

Roast Pheasant with Pancetta, White Wine and Rosemary

Arrosto di fagiano con pancetta, vino bianco e rosmarino

Serves 4

This is an impressive yet simple dish for entertaining. I like dishes that I don't have to stand over when I have guests round. That way, I'm free to enjoy my visitors' company. If pheasant is unavailable, this works wonderfully with chicken – just add a couple more pancetta slices.

extra virgin olive oil
4 sprigs of rosemary, leaves chopped
1 lemon, zested then sliced
1 x 1kg pheasant
salt and freshly ground black pepper
4 slices pancetta
200ml white wine
chicory roasted with Parmesan (p. 199), to serve

1. Preheat the oven to 180°C.
2. Mix together some olive oil, some of the rosemary and all of the lemon zest, then brush it over the pheasant. Season the cavity with the remaining rosemary, salt and pepper and a few slices of lemon. Cover the breast area with the pancetta. Place in a roasting tin and pour over the white wine.
3. Roast for 1 hour, basting from time to time. Lower the heat to 150°C and cook for up to another 30 minutes, or until tender and cooked through and the juices run clear when the thigh is pierced.
4. Remove from the pan and place on a serving plate to rest, then pour the juices on top. Serve with chicory roasted with Parmesan (p. 199).

✳ Add about 12 olives and use Marsala instead of the wine for a change. Add double cream to the juices for a richer sauce.

Sides

Potato and Parmesan Gratin
Gratin di patate e Parmigiano

Potato and Tomato Bake
Patate e pomodoro al forno

Garlic and Sage Roast Potatoes
Patate al forno con aglio e salvia

Beans, Maruzzara Style
Fagioli alla Maruzzara

Baked Fennel with Lemon and Olives
Finocchi al forno con limone e olive

Roasted Pumpkin with Shallots and Orange
Zucca al forno con scalogni e arancne

Sautéed Broccoli
Broccoli saltati

Chicory Roasted with Parmesan
Endiva al forno con Parmigiano

Oven-baked Asparagus
Asparagi al forno

Roman (Jewish-style) Fried Artichokes
Carciofi alla Giudia

Potato and Parmesan Gratin

Gratin di patate e Parmigiano

Serves 6

This is a rich dish that's excellent with fish and stews. To lighten the recipe, replace half the cream with chicken or vegetable stock. The Parmesan can also be replaced with grated Gruyère, mozzarella or even cheddar cheese.

1kg potatoes, peeled and thinly sliced (I use Roosters or Kerrs Pink in season)
salt and freshly ground black pepper
100g freshly grated Parmesan
500ml double cream

1. Preheat the oven to 180°C.
2. Butter a square 20cm baking tin (or lasagne dish). Arrange a layer of sliced potatoes on the bottom of the tin. Season the potatoes with a little salt and pepper and sprinkle with some of the Parmesan. Repeat this process of layering until all the potatoes are in the tin, using the last of the cheese on the top.
3. Place on a baking tray lined with foil, then pour the cream over the surface. Bake in the oven for 2 hours. Using the back of a spatula, keep pressing the potatoes down from time to time. When the potatoes are tender and the surface is crisp and golden brown, the gratin is ready for serving.

* If you enjoy this type of dish, it's worth investing in a mandolin for preparing wonderfully thin slices of potatoes with minimum effort. Also, covering the baking tray with foil really does help keep your oven clean.

* You could precook the potatoes as in the potato and tomato bake (p. 191) to shorten the cooking time in the oven.

Potato and Tomato Bake

Patate e pomodoro al forno

Serves 6

For a lighter gratin, this is the recipe for you. The potato works surprisingly well with the tomatoes – but the tomatoes must be red and ripe. Very thinly sliced fennel or roasted red peppers or sweet potato are good alternatives to the tomatoes.

1kg potatoes, peeled
100ml milk
3 garlic cloves, sliced
1 tsp fennel seeds, lightly crushed
½ tsp saffron
salt and freshly ground black pepper

3 large ripe tomatoes, sliced
120ml vegetable stock
4 tbsp white breadcrumbs
4 tbsp freshly grated Parmesan
2 tbsp extra virgin olive oil

1. Place the potatoes in a saucepan, cover with water, bring to the boil and simmer for 5–6 minutes. Drain, then slice thinly once they're cool enough to handle.
2. Preheat the oven to 180°C. Butter a square 20cm baking tin (or lasagne dish).
3. Mix the milk, garlic, fennel seeds, saffron, salt and pepper in a bowl.
4. Start by layering the potatoes in the bottom of the tin. Drizzle a little of the milk and saffron mixture over. Cover with a layer of tomatoes, then a layer of potatoes and so on. Finally, pour over the stock.
5. Mix the breadcrumbs with the Parmesan and sprinkle over, then drizzle over the extra virgin olive oil.
6. Bake for about 1 ½ hours. Using the back of a spatula, keep pressing the potatoes down from time to time. When the potatoes are tender and the surface is crisp and golden brown, the gratin is ready for serving.

✻ By precooking the potatoes, the cooking time in the oven will be shortened. This could also be done for the potato and Parmesan gratin (p. 190).

Garlic and Sage Roast Potatoes

Patate al forno con aglio e salvia

Serves 4 **E**

My children love this recipe made with baby Charlotte potatoes, halved, with the skins still on. I've also replaced the white potatoes with sweet potatoes, which is lovely and cooks even faster.

6–8 large floury potatoes, peeled and cut in half
sea salt and freshly ground black pepper
5 tbsp extra virgin olive oil
12 sage leaves
7–8 garlic cloves

1. Preheat the oven to 220°C.
2. Parboil the potatoes for 12 minutes, then drain and sprinkle with salt.
3. Heat the olive oil in a roasting tin. Toss the potatoes, sage leaves, garlic and pepper into the pan and roast for 30–35 minutes. Turn the potatoes after 15 minutes to ensure they are crispy all over.

✳ Try rosemary instead of the sage and try this dish with goose fat instead of the olive oil.

Beans, Maruzzara Style

Fagioli alla Maruzzara

Serves 4

*I was never really into cooking with beans until I met Claudio, and now I'm a true convert.
We had the most memorable of bean dishes as a side order dining in the shade on a hot
sunny day, sipping the local wine at a small village trattoria near Montepulciano.
This recipe is close to the original; the weather I shall leave to a higher authority.*

Depending on where you are in Italy, beans will appear in various dishes, such as Pasta e
Fagioli *(beans with pasta) or a simple soup. This recipe is from the Campania region, and if you
added some vegetable or chicken stock and grated Parmesan, it would make a hearty soup.*

300g dried white cannellini beans
1 tsp bicarbonate of soda
2 celery stalks, finely sliced
300g tinned whole cherry tomatoes
75ml extra virgin olive oil
2 garlic cloves, crushed
2 tbsp chopped parsley, plus extra to garnish
½ tsp dried oregano
salt and freshly ground black pepper

1. Soak the beans overnight in cold water mixed with the bicarbonate of soda. Rinse well
    and place in a pot. Cover with water and bring to the boil, then simmer for 25 minutes.
2. Add the celery and simmer for 15 minutes. Add the tomatoes, olive oil, garlic, parsley
    and oregano. Bring to the boil and simmer for 5 minutes. Check the seasoning.
    Garnish with more chopped parsley and serve with belly of pork (p. 176) or some
    grilled fish.

✳ Using bicarbonate of soda is a handy tip in this recipe, as it
softens the skin of the beans while soaking. And it's important to
barely simmer the beans, otherwise they can break up a little.

Baked Fennel with Lemon and Olives

Finocchi al forno con limone e olive

Serves 4

Fennel is a surprisingly versatile vegetable. It can be shaved into thin slices in a salad (like in the scallop dish on p. 29), roasted, baked, used in a risotto (see the recipe for lemon chicken on p. 162) and as a base for sauces. At a spring Sunday lunch in the Fulvio household in Palermo, fennel, in season at this time, is the vegetable to follow the meat course. Fennel bulbs are passed around the table and we pull off a layer and munch – no dressing, no seasoning, just simple fennel with its distinct aniseed flavour to cleanse the palate.

3 large or 4 medium fennel bulbs
zest of 1 lemon
juice of ½ lemon
100ml extra virgin olive oil
salt and freshly ground black pepper
12 black or green olives

1. Preheat the oven to 200°C.
2. Trim the fennel and cut away any bruised parts. Keep the fronds for garnish later. Cut off the fibrous tops, halve the bulbs lengthways and cut out the core. Cut larger bulbs into quarters. Place the fennel halves or quarters in a baking dish, cut side up.
3. Mix the lemon zest and juice with the olive oil, salt and pepper. Pour the lemon and olive oil mixture over the fennel and bake in the oven for 15 minutes. Turn the fennel, add the olives and bake for a further 15 minutes. Turn once more and bake for a final 15 minutes, until tender. Serve sprinkled with the fennel fronds.

* For a softer texture, blanch the fennel halves or quarters in boiling water for 2 minutes and drain well before baking.

194

*Garlic and sage roast
potatoes (top left),
sautéed broccoli (right)
and roasted pumpkin
with shallots and
orange (bottom)*

Roasted Pumpkin with Shallots and Orange

Zucca al forno con scalogni e arancne

Serves 6 Ⓔ

Oranges may not spring to mind as a flavouring for roast vegetables, but it gives a wonderful subtle flavour to this recipe. I always roast the orange shell with the vegetables too, for additional flavour.

1 small pumpkin
8 shallots, halved
1 orange, halved crossways and juiced
4 tbsp extra virgin olive oil
2 large sprigs of rosemary
salt and freshly ground black pepper
6 garlic cloves, left whole

1. Preheat the oven to 200°C.
2. Cut the pumpkin in half, scoop out the seeds with a metal spoon and discard. Cut the pumpkin into wedges, leaving the skin on.
3. Put the pumpkin and shallots into a large roasting tin. Squeeze over the orange juice and put the squeezed halves into the tin with the vegetables. Drizzle with the olive oil and put the rosemary sprigs on top. Add salt and pepper and roast for 30 minutes.
4. Remove from the oven and add the garlic. Shake the pan to prevent the vegetables from sticking. Return the pan to the oven for a further 15 minutes, until the vegetables are tender and slightly caramelised.

✳ Use butternut squash or parsnips as an alternative.
    Thyme also wells very well in this recipe.

Sautéed Broccoli

Broccoli saltati

Serves 4

Steamed broccoli can be so plain and, dare I say, even boring. The hot balsamic dressing lifts this dish. Romanesco is a lovely sweet-tasting broccoli that resembles half cauliflower, half broccoli and the flowers grow into a point in the centre. Replace the broccoli with asparagus as an alternative.

1kg tender stem broccoli or regular broccoli, Romanesco or Sicilian purple
4 tbsp extra virgin olive oil
2 garlic cloves, thinly sliced
1 tbsp balsamic vinegar
salt and freshly ground black pepper

1. If using the tender stem broccoli, simply steam or blanch the broccoli for 3–5 minutes until al dente. With regular broccoli, first cut the broccoli into florets and peel and slice the remaining stem before steaming for 4–6 minutes.
2. Meanwhile, heat the oil in a pan. Add the garlic, balsamic vinegar, salt and pepper and sauté lightly for 2–3 minutes. Pour this sauce over the broccoli to serve.

✳ Try adding 2 or 3 mashed anchovy fillets or a chopped red chilli when you add the vinegar.

Chicory Roasted with Parmesan

Endiva al forno con Parmigiano

Serves 4 Ⓔ

Chicory, or Belgian endive, as it's also known, is another of those more unusual but very versatile ingredients. In season in spring, it's wonderfully crispy in a salad. We also use it as a pizza topping (see p. 61), and here it's roasted for a delicious and impressive side dish.

extra virgin olive oil
3–4 chicory
salt and freshly ground black pepper
3 tbsp freshly grated Parmesan, plus extra shavings to garnish

1. Preheat the oven to 180°C. Brush an ovenproof dish with some olive oil.
2. Blanch the chicory for 1–2 minutes in boiling water, then drain on kitchen paper. Place the chicory in the dish, season with salt and pepper and sprinkle over the grated Parmesan. Bake for about 15 minutes, until the chicory is cooked through and lightly golden in colour. Drizzle with a little olive oil and sprinkle over the Parmesan shavings.

✳ I especially like to serve this with fish, as chicory's distinct flavour works well with the subtlety of fish.

Oven-baked Asparagus

Asparagi al forno

Serves 4

This recipe is perfect not only as a side, but also as a starter when served with a cream sauce or a Gorgonzola sauce (p. 80). When asparagus is out of season, substitute green beans.

24 asparagus spears
4 slices Parma ham
20g butter, melted
40g freshly grated Parmesan cheese
3 tbsp breadcrumbs
2 tsp chopped parsley

1. Preheat the oven to 180°C. Grease an ovenproof dish or baking tray.
2. Trim and clean the asparagus (see tip below). Cook in simmering water for about 3–4 minutes, until just al dente, then drain and allow to cool.
3. Take 6 asparagus spears and wrap them in a slice of Parma ham. Repeat with the remaining spears. Lay all the spears in the ovenproof dish or baking tray. Pour over the melted butter and sprinkle with the Parmesan, breadcrumbs and parsley. Bake for 5–10 minutes, until golden brown.

✳ To prepare asparagus, snap off the woody part at the base of the stem. For perfect presentation, trim the snapped end and using a vegetable peeler, shape to a point to match the top.

Roman (Jewish-style) Fried Artichokes

Carciofi alla Giudia

Serves 4

It might take a little time and practice to prepare an artichoke, but it's worth it for sheer flavour. Rather than deep frying, I sometimes steam the artichokes for a lighter option.

4 artichokes
juice of 1 lemon
olive oil
sea salt
lemon dressing (p. 181), to serve

1. First clean the artichokes by pulling off the tough outer leaves. You'll see the pale yellow leaves below. Using a vegetable peeler, peel the stems and trim to about 3cm. With a sharp knife, trim about 2cm off of the tops. Using scissors, cut the sharp, thorny tips off the leaves. Using a spoon, scoop out the fibrous white choke.
2. Drizzle lemon juice over the artichokes to prevent them from going brown, but be sure to pat them dry before frying, otherwise the oil will spit.
3. Heat a deep saucepan with oil or preheat the deep fryer to 190°C. (It must be very hot but not smoking.) Place the artichokes into the oil and fry for 7–8 minutes, or until they are golden brown and the stem is tender. Place the artichoke flower, stem side up, onto kitchen paper and allow to drain.
4. Transfer onto a presentation platter. Sprinkle with sea salt and serve with a lemon dressing (p. 181).

* If you have quite a few artichokes to prepare, have a bowl of lemon water ready and put the artichokes in the bowl, cut side down in the water, to prevent browning.
Dry them well before deep frying.

Desserts, Cakes, Biscuits and Drinks

Sponge Cake Filled with Ricotta, Chocolate
and Candied Fruit
Cassata

Apple Cake with Olive Oil
Torta di miele all'olio d'oliva

Raspberry Tiramisù
Tiramisù ai lamponi

Amaretto and Almond Truffle Torte
Torta di cioccolato e amaretto

Hazelnut and Orange Honey Tart
Crostata alle nocciole e miele d'arancia

Plum and Mascarpone Tart
Crostata di prugne e mascarpone

Meringues with Ricotta Cream and Balsamic Strawberries
Meringhe con crema di ricotta e fragole balsamico

Marsala Custard
Zabaglione

Orange Hearts
Cuori d'arancia

Yoghurt Panna Cotta

Baked Stuffed Peaches with Amaretti
Pesche al forno ripiene con amaretti

Amaretti Biscuits
Amaretti

Carnival Biscuits
Chiacchere

Lemon and Pine Nut Biscotti
Biscotti al limone e pinoli

Frozen Desserts
Dolci freddi

Lemon Granita
Granita al limone

Iced Cream of Coffee
Crema al Caffé

Ice Cream
Gelati

Basic Ice Cream – Strawberry, Pistachio, Chocolate and Stem Ginger
Fragola, pistacchio, cioccolato, zenzero

Carpaccio of Pineapple and Coconut Ice Cream
Carpaccio di ananas con gelato al cocco

Limoncello, White Chocolate and Cherry Semifreddo
Semifreddo al limoncello, cioccolata bianca e cilege

Ice Cream Drowned in Coffee
Affogato al Caffé

Drinks

Limoncello

Bellini

Amaretto, Catherine Style

Sponge Cake Filled with Ricotta, Chocolate and Candied Fruit

Cassata

Serves 12

Apparently in sixteenth-century Sicily, the nuns were banned from making cassata, as it kept them from their prayers, so I've developed this faster version of the recipe so as not to delay anyone unnecessarily in the kitchen!

There are a number of forms of cassata – baked, ice cream and cake. The cake is traditional in Palermo and is finished with green icing and white piping. Most people would buy a cassata in their local bakery and it's a particular favourite as a grand finale for Sunday lunch.

for the cake:
5 large eggs, separated
½ tsp salt
375g caster sugar, divided
zest of 1 lemon
325g flour
1 tsp baking powder

for the filling:
350g ricotta
150g icing sugar
¼ tsp cinnamon
60g dark chocolate chips
60g candied fruits, such as cherries,
    pineapple, apricot and papaya
50g pine nuts, toasted
100ml Marsala

for the syrup:
100ml orange juice
100ml Marsala

for the icing and decoration:
200g ricotta
500g icing sugar
flaked almonds, toasted
candied fruits (we used candied slices of
    oranges and lemons for decoration)

1. Preheat the oven to 180°C. Line, butter and flour a 23cm springform cake tin.
2. To make the cake, beat the egg whites until stiff peaks form, then fold in the salt and 100g caster sugar.

3. In a separate bowl, beat the egg yolks with the remaining 275g sugar and the lemon zest. Carefully fold the yolk and sugar mixture into the whites.

4. Sieve the flour with the baking powder and fold into the egg mixture. Pour the mixture into the prepared cake tin and bake for approximately 55 minutes, until a skewer inserted into the middle comes out clean. Allow to cool.

5. Meanwhile, to make the filling, combine all the ingredients and set aside.

6. To make the syrup, combine the orange juice and Marsala and set aside.

7. To assemble the cake once it has cooled, using a serrated knife, cut across the cake twice to form three layers. Sprinkle the cut half of each layer with the orange juice and Marsala syrup. Lay out some cling film and put the base of the cake in the centre. Spread the filling between each layer. Wrap cling film over the cake and place the cake back in the springform tin, pressing down to compress lightly. Chill for 6 hours.

8. Meanwhile, to make the icing, whisk the ricotta and icing sugar together. Set aside.

9. To complete the *cassata*, unmould the cake and place on a platter. Ice the top and sides of the cake with the ricotta icing. Decorate the sides with the toasted almond flakes and the top with the candied fruit.

* I usually get ahead with this recipe by preparing the cake the night before and filling and icing it the next day.

* To candy fruit, simply put equal parts sugar and water in a saucepan and simmer until the mixture is quite syrupy, then add in thinly sliced orange and lemon segments, with the rind still on, and simmer for about 15 minutes. Remove from the syrup (careful, as they will be hot) and allow them to cool and set on baking parchment.

Apple Cake with Olive Oil

Torta di miele all'olio d'oliva

Serves 8–10

This is a lovely cake from the north of Italy, where interestingly, olive oil replaces butter in the recipe. The apple softens in the baking process, resulting in a wonderfully moist cake. The flavours are very autumnal, and in fact, I have made this as my alternative Christmas cake.

110g golden raisins or sultanas
200g golden caster sugar
3 large eggs
150ml extra virgin olive oil
350g plain flour
1 tsp ground cinnamon
½ tsp ground ginger

1 tsp bicarbonate of soda
1 tsp baking powder
pinch of salt
zest of 1 lemon
500g cooking apples, peeled and diced into
   1 ½ cm pieces

1. Preheat the oven to 180°C. Butter and flour a 20cm springform cake tin.
2. Place the raisins or sultanas in a bowl of hot water and allow to soak for 15 minutes to plump up. Drain and set aside.
3. Whisk the sugar and eggs until doubled in volume and pale cream in colour. Warm the olive oil in a saucepan, then slowly whisk it into the eggs and sugar.
4. Sieve the flour, cinnamon, ginger, bicarbonate of soda, baking powder and salt, then gradually add to the oil and egg mixture. Fold in well.
5. Add the drained raisins to the mixture, along with the lemon zest and diced apples. Mix thoroughly. The mixture should be stiff at this stage.
6. Spoon the mixture into the prepared cake tin. Bake for at least 1 hour, until a skewer inserted in the middle comes out clean. Carefully remove the cake from the tin and allow to cool on a wire rack.

✳ As a delicious alternative to the apples, try diced pear.

Raspberry Tiramisù

Tiramisù ai lamponi

Serves 8–10

What a luxurious dessert. Invented in Venice, tiramisù *means 'pick me up'. The original recipe is made with espresso and Marsala, but I have my own delicious twist by introducing raspberries and orange. It's equally tasty made with strawberries.*

300g raspberry jam
75ml plus 4 tbsp Marsala or sherry
150ml orange juice
475g mascarpone, at room temperature
375ml chilled whipping cream

60g caster sugar
1 tsp vanilla extract
52 savoiardi biscuits (approx.)
600g raspberries, divided

1. Whisk the jam, 75ml Marsala and the orange juice together. Set aside.
2. Place the mascarpone cheese and 2 tbsp Marsala in a large bowl. Fold just to blend and set aside.
3. Beat the cream, sugar, vanilla and the remaining 2 tbsp Marsala in another large bowl until soft peaks form.
4. Stir a quarter of the whipped cream mixture into the mascarpone mixture to loosen it, then gently fold in the remaining whipped cream.
5. Spread some of the jam mixture in the bottom of a 32cm x 22cm x 12cm serving dish (or you can use individual glasses). Arrange enough savoiardi over the jam mixture to cover the bottom of the dish. Spoon more of the jam mixture over the savoiardi, then spread some of the mascarpone mixture over. Arrange some raspberries over the mascarpone mixture.
6. Repeat the layering with the remaining savoiardi, jam mixture, mascarpone mixture and raspberries. Cover with cling film and chill for at least 8 hours or overnight. Arrange any leftover raspberries over the *tiramisù* and serve.

* If possible, it's best to prepare this a day ahead so all the elements can meld and the savoiardi can soften fully. Ladyfingers can be used instead of savoiardi, but they are less effective in soaking up the lovely juices.

Amaretto and Almond Truffle Torte

Torta di cioccolato e amaretto

Serves 12

As chocolate is one of the loves of my life, this cake is regularly rustled up at home. It's incredibly easy to make – though you do need an electric whisk to get the volume with the eggs – but is so rich and yet so light.

If by some chance there happens to be leftovers, keep this cake at room temperature and enjoy it within 3 days. Refrigeration will cause the chocolate and butter to harden.

1 tbsp flour
6 large eggs, at room temperature
6 tbsp caster sugar
150g butter
2 tbsp amaretto
350g bittersweet chocolate, chopped
60g ground almonds, lightly toasted
icing sugar, to decorate
mascarpone or whipped cream, to serve

1. Preheat the oven to 180°C. Generously butter a 23cm springform cake tin and lightly dust with the flour. Turn the pan upside down and shake out the excess flour. Wrap two layers of aluminium foil around the outside of the bottom of the cake tin.
2. Beat the eggs and sugar with an electric mixer at top speed for 8–10 minutes, until they become light and turn a cream colour, with lots of volume.
3. Meanwhile, melt the butter in a small saucepan and stir in the amaretto. Set aside.
4. Pour about 5cm hot water in a large saucepan and keep it at a simmer. Place a mixing bowl (preferably ceramic) on top of the saucepan, ensuring that the base of the bowl does not touch the water.
5. Add the melted butter mixture and the chocolate to the bowl and stir until the chocolate is completely melted. Remove the bowl immediately and allow to cool slightly.

6. Meanwhile, toast the ground almonds, heat a dry frying pan over a medium heat. Add the nuts and stir until they are golden. Set aside.

7. Fold one-third of the egg mixture into the chocolate mixture, then pour this mix back in with the remaining two-thirds of the egg. Add the almonds and fold very gently until the chocolate and egg are incorporated. It's important not to overmix in order to keep as much air as possible in the batter. Pour the mixture into the prepared cake tin.

8. Sit the tin into a deep baking tray to form a bain marie and place in the preheated oven. Pour in enough hot water to come about one-third up the sides of the cake tin. Bake for 25–30 minutes. When ready, the top of the cake will lose its glossiness, will be slightly wobbly in the centre and an inserted skewer should come out gooey. It should not bake so long that it cracks.

9. Let the cake cool completely in its tin on a wire rack. Run a small knife around the edge of the cake to remove the outer ring. Dust the top of the cake with icing sugar and serve with mascarpone or whipped cream.

* Replace the amaretto with Baileys or simply the grated zest of an orange and flavour the accompanying mascarpone or cream with the same ingredients for maximum effect.

Hazelnut and Orange Honey Tart

Crostata alle nocciole e miele d'arancia

Serves 8

Hazelnuts are abundant, yet valuable in the Nebrodi Mountains of Sicily. Tullio Scurrio told me of his experiences collecting hazelnuts as a child in the area. An elderly lady owned the field with the main crop of hazelnuts in his village. When the nuts were ready for picking, she would hang her white laundry on the clothesline as a signal for the villagers to come and collect them. An armed man on a mule would guard the field by night, such was (and still is) their value.

Tullio had me eating hazelnut ice cream in a brioche bun for breakfast and it made a great change from toast, so it might yet catch on in the Fulvio household.

for the pastry:
225g plain flour
110g cold butter, diced
zest of 1 orange
30g icing sugar
1 egg
1 tbsp cold orange juice or water

for the filling:
150g hazelnuts, toasted, skinned
    and chopped
2 eggs
75g caster sugar
pinch of salt
zest and juice of 1 small orange
100g honey
75g unsalted butter, diced
icing sugar, to decorate

1. Preheat the oven to 180°C. Butter a 23cm x 2 ½cm loose-bottomed tart tin.
2. To make the pastry, sieve the flour into a bowl. Add the diced butter and rub it in with your fingertips until the mixture resembles breadcrumbs. Add the orange zest, then sieve in the icing sugar and stir.
3. Beat the egg with the orange juice (or water) and add to the flour. Mix until it forms a firm dough. Wrap in cling film and refrigerate for 20 minutes to let the dough rest before rolling.
4. Flour a work surface and roll out the pastry slightly bigger than the tin. Line the tin with the pastry and prick the base with a fork. Place in the fridge to rest for approximately 10 minutes. Remove from the fridge and line with parchment paper, then fill with baking beans or rice. Place in the preheated oven for 10 minutes.

5. Meanwhile, to make the filling, first toast the hazelnuts. Heat a dry frying pan over a medium heat. Add the nuts and stir until golden. Remove the skins by placing the nuts in a clean tea towel, gathering the four corners of the towel and rubbing the hazelnuts. Chop the nuts and set aside.
6. Whisk the eggs and caster sugar together. Mix in the salt, orange zest and juice and stir well.
7. Place the honey and butter in a small saucepan and heat gently, then add to the egg and sugar mixture.
8. Remove the parchment and baking beans from the tart case. Spread the hazelnuts over the base and pour in the egg mixture.
9. Bake for approximately 45 minutes, or until the filling is light brown in colour and has set. Place on a wire rack to cool slightly. Dust lightly with icing sugar and serve warm.

✳ Try lemon and pine nut as an alternative to hazelnut and orange.

Plum and Mascarpone Tart

Crostata di prugne e mascarpone

Makes 1 large tart or 6 individual tartlets, serves 6–8

Once the pastry is made, this is actually a particularly easy recipe. I also make this same tart with fresh strawberries or raspberries and it looks and tastes beautiful for a summer party.

for the pastry:
225g plain flour
110g cold butter, diced
30g icing sugar
1 egg
1 tbsp cold water

for the filling:
450g fresh plums,
    stoned and quartered
1 tbsp brown sugar
400g mascarpone
240ml double cream

2 tsp caster sugar
1 tbsp sherry
icing sugar, to decorate
sprig of mint, to decorate

1. Preheat the oven to 180°C. Butter a 23cm x 2 ½cm loose-bottomed tart tin or 6 individual tartlet tins.
2. To make the pastry, sieve the flour into a bowl. Add the diced butter and rub it in with your fingertips until the mixture resembles breadcrumbs. Sieve in the icing sugar and stir.
3. Beat the egg with the water and add to the flour. Mix until it forms a firm dough. Wrap in cling film and refrigerate for 20 minutes to let the dough rest before rolling.
4. Flour a work surface and roll out the pastry slightly bigger than the tin. Line the tin with the pastry and prick the base with a fork. Place in the fridge to rest for approximately 10 minutes. Remove from the fridge, line with parchment paper and fill with baking beans or rice. Place in the preheated oven for 10–15 minutes, until fully baked. Set aside.
5. Place the plums on a baking tray and sprinkle with the brown sugar. Bake in the preheated oven for 15 minutes, until they are cooked but still hold their shape. Allow to cool.
6. Mix the mascarpone with the cream, sugar and sherry. Refrigerate until needed.
7. Just prior to serving, spoon the mascarpone into the cooked pastry shell and place the plums on top, making them look as pretty as you can. Dust with a little icing sugar and decorate with a sprig of mint.

✳ We have an abundance of gooseberries in our garden, so I simmer them gently with a dash of elderflower syrup and sugar. When cooled, I replace the plums in this recipe with the gooseberries and it's so delicious.

Meringues with a Ricotta Cream and Balsamic Strawberries

Meringhe con crema di ricotta e fragole balsamico

Serves 6

Mmm, meringues. Such a delightful summer dessert brimming with fresh fruit – I love them. Strawberries and balsamic vinegar may seem like a strange pairing, but it really works, honestly! The only important note is to strain the strawberries well before serving and discard the balsamic mix.

for the meringues:
3 egg whites
170g caster sugar
pinch of salt
½ tsp white wine vinegar
½ tsp cornflour

for the balsamic strawberries:
200g strawberries, hulled
50g light brown sugar
1 ½ tbsp balsamic vinegar
½ tsp salt

for the ricotta cream:
100ml double cream
120g ricotta
20g icing sugar, plus extra to decorate
zest of 1 lemon

mint leaves, to decorate

1. Preheat the oven to 140°C. Line a baking sheet with parchment paper.
2. Tip the egg whites with the salt into a large, spotlessly clean mixing bowl. Beat them on medium speed until the mixture resembles soft peaks. Turn the speed up and start to add the sugar a spoonful at a time. Continue beating for 3–4 seconds between each addition. Fold in the vinegar and the cornflour. The mixture should be smooth and glossy.
3. Fill a piping bag with the egg white mixture and create the shape that you prefer on the lined baking sheet, such as hearts or circles, creating an edge to the meringue by piping small rosettes around the sides. Bake immediately for 1 hour, or until crisp and dry. Allow to cool completely.

4. To prepare the strawberries, mix them with the brown sugar, vinegar and salt. Refrigerate for about 30 minutes, then mix again. Allow to macerate for about 2 hours.
5. Meanwhile, to prepare the ricotta filling, whisk the cream until it forms soft peaks and gently fold into the ricotta. Sieve the icing sugar and slowly add into the ricotta mixture, together with the lemon zest.
6. Fill the cooled meringues with the lemon ricotta cream. Strain the strawberries and place on top. Decorate with mint leaves and a dusting of icing sugar to serve.

✳ For a richer filling, replace the ricotta with mascarpone.

Marsala Custard

Zabaglione

Serves 4

Originating in Venice, this is a simple and elegant dessert, especially if served in decorative glasses. The classic recipe has raw eggs, but I like to cook out the eggs over a bain marie. The key ingredient here is Marsala. If unavailable, try Madeira or a sweet sherry.

8 egg yolks (or 5 egg yolks and 2 whole eggs)
150g sugar
100ml Marsala
thin strips of orange peel, to decorate

1. Place the egg yolks and sugar into a large bowl and whisk until thick and pale yellow, about 4 minutes. Set the egg mixture over a bain marie and gradually drizzle in the Marsala, whisking all the time.
2. Continue whisking until the mixture doubles in volume and is holding soft peaks, about 12–15 minutes. Do not let the eggs set around the edges of the bowl.
3. Spoon into 4 glasses and decorate with orange peel. Serve warm or chilled.

※ I like to serve zabaglione with orange biscuits (see p. 226) and some figs or summer berries.

Orange Hearts

Cuori d'arancia

Makes 18–20 biscuits

This is quite a versatile recipe, as the biscuits work well sandwiched around fruits, such as poached pears, with ice cream or simply with a good cup of Italian coffee.

180g white flour
60g caster sugar
zest and juice of 1 orange
120g butter

1. Preheat the oven to 180°C. Lightly flour a baking tray or line with parchment paper.
2. Put the flour, sugar and orange zest into a bowl, then rub in the butter fully until the mixture resembles breadcrumbs. Work the mixture together to form a ball, adding just enough orange juice to bind. Knead the dough a little in the bowl, then dust the work surface with flour and place the dough on top. Flour a rolling pin and roll the dough out until it's 5–7mm thick.
3. Cut into hearts or your preferred shape. Place carefully on the lined baking tray. Bake for about 10–12 minutes, until pale brown. Remove and cool on a wire rack.

✱ Try ½ tsp ground cinnamon or ginger instead of the orange zest, or drizzle with melted chocolate when cooled.

Yoghurt Panna Cotta

Serves 4

This is an Irish take on panna cotta, *which means 'cooked cream'. I also make it with buttermilk rather than yoghurt. I find the sharpness of either cuts through the rich creaminess of the classic recipe.*

185ml cream
50g caster sugar
½ vanilla pod, split lengthways
1 ½ gelatine leaves
250g natural yoghurt

1. Place the cream and sugar in a saucepan over a medium heat.
2. Using the point of a knife, scrape the vanilla seeds into the saucepan before adding the entire bean. Stir until the sugar is dissolved, then bring to the boil before removing from the heat. Remove the vanilla pod.
3. Soak the gelatine in cold water for about 2 minutes, until soft. Squeeze out the excess water and drop the gelatine into the hot cream mixture and whisk until dissolved. Add the yoghurt and whisk until smooth.
4. Strain the mixture through a fine sieve and divide between 4 x 125ml ramekins, cappuccino cups, martini glasses or white wine glasses. Cover with cling film and chill for at least 3 hours, or until set. Bring to room temperature before serving.

* To remove the panna cotta from the ramekins, dip the base
    of them in hot water for only a few seconds, then invert
onto a serving plate.

* Panna cotta is delicious with fresh fruit, especially
    raspberries, strawberries or rhubarb in season.

Baked Stuffed Peaches with Amaretti

Pesche al forno ripiene con amaretti

Serves 4

Apricots and nectarines as an alternative to peaches are a firm family favourite. This dessert is a light option to follow a heavy meal. It works well in my household, as it's another way to entice the children to enjoy more fruit (without the amaretto, of course).

butter, for greasing
4 peaches
5 amaretti biscuits
1 egg yolk
1 tsp sugar
1 tbsp amaretto
mascarpone or cream, to serve

1. Preheat the oven to 200°C. Grease a baking tray with butter.
2. Halve the peaches and remove the stones. Scoop out some flesh with a melon baller and place into a bowl.
3. Place the biscuits in a plastic bag and crush them with a rolling pin. Mix the biscuits, egg yolk, sugar and amaretto with the peach flesh.
4. Place the peaches on the greased baking tray. Spoon the amaretti mix into the peaches.
5. Bake for 15–20 minutes. Serve with mascarpone or cream.

* You could also serve this with a sweet sauce made from 150ml orange juice, a dash of sherry and 4 tbsp raspberry jam. Bring this to a simmer and allow to thicken slightly.

Amaretti Biscuits

Amaretti

Makes 40 biscuits

These are typically given for free with a coffee in any coffee bar, but the home-made ones totally surpass the freebies. When I make these, one is not enough … actually, make that ten. They are also delicious served with vanilla ice cream and a raspberry coulis for dessert.

butter, for greasing
4 egg whites
350g caster sugar
1 ½ tbsp amaretto
350g ground almonds

1. Preheat the oven to 180°C. Place some baking parchment on a baking tray and butter lightly.
2. In a large bowl, beat the egg whites until stiff. Gently mix in the sugar, amaretto and almonds. Using a teaspoon, place small dollops (about 2cm) onto the sheet.
3. Bake for 12–15 minutes, until a pale golden brown. Leave to set on the baking tray, as they are quite soft at this stage. They will harden as they cool.

＊ Melt some chocolate and whip some cream. When the chocolate has cooled slightly and the cream is at room temperature, fold them together and use to sandwich two amaretti together for the ultimate biscuit.

Carnival Biscuits

Chiacchere

Makes 24 biscuits

My friend Solina Testagrossa, who has a lovely bakery (panifico) in our local town of Ballestrate, taught me this recipe. These are special deep-fried sweet treats that are made only for the celebration of Carnevale, which is a huge carnival celebration in the lead-up to Lent and the odd person out is the one who isn't in fancy dress.

160ml white wine
20g sugar
1 tsp dried yeast (or 1 x 7g sachet)
500g strong white flour
1 tbsp honey
1 litre oil, for deep frying
icing sugar, to decorate

1. Gently heat the wine in a saucepan. It should be warm, not hot. Remove from the heat and add the sugar and yeast to it. Set aside and leave the yeast to activate.
2. Sieve the flour into a bowl. Make a well in the centre of the flour and add the honey. When the yeast is activated, add the wine mix slowly to the flour, mixing with one hand. When all the wine mix has been added, the dough should be soft.
3. Knead very gently for 2 minutes, then leave to rest for 15 minutes.
4. Meanwhile, heat the oil for frying. Flour a work surface. Using a rolling pin, roll out the dough to ½cm thick. Using a pastry cutter, cut out rectangles roughly 8cm x 6cm. Cut a 4cm strip down the centre and pull apart slightly.
5. Deep fry immediately after cutting for 2 minutes in total, until golden brown. Remove from the oil with a slotted spoon, place on kitchen paper for about 20 seconds and then sprinkle with icing sugar.

✲ Don't be too concerned about the shape as described above. This recipe is particular to the wonderful Solina, but it's also possible to cut them into triangles or circles.

Lemon and Pine Nut Biscotti

Biscotti al limone e pinoli

Makes 20 biscotti

Biscotti are crisp, dry Italian biscuits, particularly popular for dunking in coffee.
Lemon and pine nut is my favourite, but there are hundreds of flavours available, from
orange to aniseed.

190g pine nuts
110g butter
170g sugar
2 eggs
2 tbsp lemon juice

2 tbsp lemon zest
475g plain flour
1 ½ tsp baking powder
pinch of salt

1. Preheat the oven to 180°C. Butter and flour a baking tray.
2. Place the pine nuts on a baking tray and place in the oven for 6–8 minutes, until golden brown. Allow to cool and set aside.
3. Reduce the oven temperature to 170°C.
4. In a mixing bowl, cream the butter and sugar together until light and fluffy. Beat in the eggs, lemon juice and zest.
5. In a separate bowl, combine the flour, baking powder and salt. Add to the butter and sugar mixture, mixing just until blended. Fold in the toasted pine nuts.
6. Place the dough on the prepared baking tray and form into a long log about 2 ½ cm high.
7. Bake in the middle of the oven for approximately 30–35 minutes, or until lightly browned and fairly firm to the touch. Remove from the oven, keeping the oven on for the next stage.
8. Place the baking tray on a cooling rack to allow the log to cool. When cooled, using two spatulas or egg slices, carefully transfer the log to a cutting board. With a serrated knife, slice diagonally at a 45-degree angle into slices about 2cm thick. Lay the slices flat on the baking tray and return to the oven for 10–15 minutes longer. Turn over once to dry them out slightly.
9. Remove from the oven and allow to cool fully on a rack. Store in an airtight container.

* These are very attractive when boxed and presented as
a Christmas gift.

Frozen Desserts

Dolci freddi

The Sicilians claim to have invented *gelati*, *granite* and *sorbetti*, but one thing is for sure –
no matter where you are in Italy, you won't be disappointed with the frozen desserts.
Gelati are the rich ice creams that come in a myriad of flavours, while *sorbetti* are more
ice-like and usually have egg white added, which gives them a silky texture. A *granita* is
simply a flavoured, frozen sweet water and is so refreshing on a hot day. A *semifreddo* is
a type of soft frozen ice cream and is usually prepared in block form and sliced to serve.

Lemon Granita

Granita al limone

Serves 4 Ⓔ Ⓕ

Antonio and Bruna, Claudio's cousins in Palermo, shared this recipe with me. It's such a
refreshing dessert or snack on a hot day. Every flavour of granita *imaginable is available,*
my favourites being lemon and mulberry. It can get so hot in southern Italy that it's quite
common to have granita *for breakfast.*

The cup measurements below are Bruna's tip, as it's so handy. Start with the dry ingredient
(the sugar) first so that you can use the same cup again for the liquids.

2 cups caster sugar
3 cups water
1 cup fresh lemon juice

1. Place the sugar and water in a saucepan. Bring to the boil and simmer for 8 minutes
    to form a sugar syrup. Cool and stir in the lemon juice. Freeze uncovered for 1 hour,
    until crystals form around the edge. Stir with a fork and return to the freezer. Repeat
    this process about 3 times.

2. Alternatively, freeze the *granita* totally, remove from the freezer and allow to defrost slightly. Place in a food processor and whizz until slushy. Fork the mix roughly and spoon into tumblers.
3. Serve immediately, as it will melt quickly. A long spoon and a straw are usually served with a *granita*.

✳ It's a good idea to freeze the serving glasses too in order to slow down the melting of the granita.

Iced Cream of Coffee

Crema al caffé

Serves 6–8

I discovered this refreshing treat on a really hot summer's morning by the sea at the Golfo di Castelemare. It's like a rich, sweet shot of caffeine and it really hits the spot. Back home, I serve it at dinner parties with a huge dollop of sambuca cream on top, which is simply sambuca, some icing sugar and cream, lightly beaten. I always use an espresso cup as the measuring tool for this recipe to ensure the ingredients are balanced.

3 tsp sugar (or more to taste)
6 espresso cups of freshly brewed espresso
3 espresso cups water
3 espresso cups cream

1. Melt the sugar with the hot espresso. Add the water and cream and freeze.
2. To serve, place in a food processor and whizz until the mixture is creamy. Serve immediately in chilled glasses or cups.

✳ The cup measurements above must be espresso cups, otherwise the caffeine hit would be well above the recommended daily limit!

Ice Cream
Gelati

The sheer delight on my children's faces when we walk into an ice cream parlour is picture perfect. And I would class myself as a big child in this situation too. The amazing array of flavours available is bewildering. I mean, have I time to try them all? From pistachio to orange, from liquorice to melon, it's so difficult to choose.

Basic Ice Cream

Serves 6 Ⓔ Ⓕ

The method is quite straightforward in this recipe, but if you're concerned that the mix might split over a direct heat, then follow the bain marie method in the recipe for carpaccio of pineapple and coconut ice cream on p. 241.

I asked Antonio, my husband's cousin, what the popular combinations among Palmertians are, who he tells me are partial to lemon and strawberry, chocolate and strawberry, chocolate and cinnamon, and watermelon and chocolate. My all-time favourite has to be the amazing bacio – hazelnut and chocolate. Delicious.

600ml milk
150ml cream
6 egg yolks
160g sugar

1. Bring the milk and cream to the boil, then remove from the heat.
2. Beat the yolks and sugar in a saucepan until fluffy. Slowly pour the heated milk and cream into the egg and sugar mixture over a very low heat. Continue stirring until the mixture thickens and coats the back of the spoon, taking care that this does not boil. Strain the mixture into a bowl and allow to cool.

3. Pour into an ice cream maker and freeze according to the manufacturer's instructions. If you don't have an ice cream maker, place the egg custard mixture into a rectangular plastic container, cover and freeze for 1 hour. Take out and whisk the mixture. Return to the freezer for about 45 minutes and whisk again. Repeat about 3 times, until a smooth ice cream forms. Allow to set for at least a further 3 hours.

Here are some ideas for flavoured *gelati*

Strawberry

Fragola

Purée 450g strawberries and add to the egg custard before placing the mixture in the ice cream maker.

Toasted pistachio

Pistacchio

Add 100g roughly chopped pistachios to the egg custard before placing in the ice cream maker.

Chocolate

Cioccolato

Add 110g roughly chopped 70% chocolate pieces to the boiled milk and cream and stir to melt, then continue with step 2 above.

Crystallised stem ginger

Zenzero

Add 30g crystallised stem ginger to the egg custard before placing in the ice cream maker.

Carpaccio of Pineapple and Coconut Ice Cream

Carpaccio di ananas con gelato al cocco

Serves 4

Pineapple and coconut are a marriage made in heaven, but for a change, sometimes I make black pepper ice cream to serve with the pineapple and it really works well. This dessert is perfect for a summer party.

250ml double cream
200ml coconut milk
5 egg yolks
150g sugar

pinch of saffron
1 pineapple, very finely sliced
a little sugar, for caramelising

1. Place the cream and coconut cream in a saucepan and gently heat until it just reaches the boiling point. Remove from the heat, then add the saffron to the hot cream. Set aside.
2. Beat the egg yolks and sugar in a bowl placed over a saucepan of simmering water (bain marie) until the mixture thickens. Pour the cream and saffron in with the egg and sugar mixture, whisking constantly until the custard thickens and coats the back of a spoon. Cool by standing the bowl in cold water and stir to prevent a 'skin' from forming.
3. Pour into an ice cream maker and freeze according to the manufacturer's instructions. If you don't have an ice cream maker, place the egg custard mixture into a rectangular plastic container, cover and freeze for 1 hour. Take out and whisk the mixture. Return to the freezer for about 45 minutes and whisk again. Repeat about 3 times, until a smooth ice cream forms. Allow to set for at least a further 3 hours.
4. Meanwhile, place the pineapple slices on a plate, sprinkle with sugar and caramelise lightly using a kitchen blow torch. Alternatively, grill the pineapple to colour the sugar. When cooled, serve with the coconut ice cream.

* If you find it a little difficult to caramelise the pineapple, try making a syrup with equal parts sugar and water. You could even add some chopped red chilli and pour this over the pineapple instead.

Limoncello, White Chocolate and Cherry Semifreddo

Semifreddo al limoncello, cioccolata bianca e cilege

Serves 8

A semifreddo can look very impressive on a presentation platter and is definitely a dessert that should be brought to the table in its entirety for maximum effect.

for the semifreddo:
100g tinned cherries, drained
85g caster sugar, divided
290ml double cream
4 tbsp limoncello (p. 245)
400ml crème fraîche
100g white chocolate chips
white chocolate curls, to serve

for the coulis:
250g tinned cherries
3 tbsp sugar
1 tbsp limoncello (p. 245)

1. Line a 1kg loaf tin (19cm x 1cm x 9cm) with cling film.
2. To make the *semifreddo*, chop the cherries, then place in a bowl with 45g sugar.
3. Whisk the cream, limoncello and the remainder of the sugar together until soft peaks form. Beat the crème fraîche slightly and fold this into the cream mixture. Fold in the cherries and add the chocolate chips. Pour into the loaf tin and smooth the top.
4. Freeze for 1 hour, uncovered, then cover with cling film and return to the freezer for 6 hours. This can be frozen for up to 3 weeks.
5. Meanwhile, to make the coulis, place the cherries, sugar and limoncello in a saucepan over a gentle heat until the sugar dissolves. Leave to cool. Place in a blender and whizz until smooth. For a finer finish, push the coulis through a sieve.
6. To serve, thaw the *semifreddo* in the fridge for 1 hour, then remove from the tin and peel off the wrap. Place on a presentation platter. Drizzle with some coulis, scattering the white chocolate curls on top. Serve in slices.

＊ If you run out of time to make the chocolate curls, simply break up a Flake chocolate bar and lightly scatter over the semifreddo.

Ice Cream Drowned in Coffee

Affogato al caffé

Serves 1

If you like coffee and you like ice cream, this is the answer to your dreams! Affogato al caffé *simply means 'drowned in coffee'. For something stronger, you could try a* caffé correcto, *meaning 'coffee corrected', as it has alcohol added. Because the dessert is so simple, it hinges on using the best ice cream and coffee available.*

1 scoop vanilla ice cream
1 shot espresso

1. Scoop the ice cream into a serving bowl, pour the hot coffee over the ice cream and serve.

✳ This also works well with chocolate ice cream.

Drinks

Limoncello

Makes 1 ¼ litres (E) (F)

Making limoncello is a lovely way to pass the time on a quiet January day when lemons are in season. Making homemade liqueurs is a national pastime in Sicily. All are made with 100% alcohol, which can be purchased in any local supermarket. This recipe is Franco's (another fab cousin), but the nearest I can get to it is using the highest-proof vodka available. Franco only has to put his hand out of his kitchen window to collect the lemons, while I depend on imports. But it's still really good.

6 large lemons, preferably unwaxed
1 litre of the highest-proof vodka available
350ml water
450g sugar

1. Wash the lemons (scrub them if they're waxed) and remove the peel using a vegetable peeler, taking care not to remove the white pith, as this will cause the limoncello to taste a little bitter.
2. Place the lemon zest and vodka in a sealed jar, such as a kilner jar. Close and leave to infuse for 2 weeks.
3. After the 2 weeks, bring the water and sugar to the boil then reduce to a simmer for 5 minutes to make a sugar syrup. Strain the lemon-infused vodka, squeezing some of the flavour from the lemon zest. Stir in the syrup and pour the limoncello into sterilised bottles. Seal well and freeze until required.

✳ Try the same recipe using oranges or mandarins. Delicious.

Bellini

Serves 6

A traditional Bellini uses Prosecco and white peaches. Invented by Giuseppe Cipriani, founder of the famous Harry's Bar in Venice, the Bellini is surely the most elegant long cocktail to grace our dinner parties. The recipe below is the authentic version, but I have also enjoyed it made with strawberry purée or with edible gold leaf floating in it – now that was impressive.

3 very ripe white peaches, peeled, destoned and roughly chopped
2 tsp sugar
1 bottle Prosecco
mint sprigs, to garnish

1. Place the peaches and sugar in a food processor and blend until smooth. Set aside in the refrigerator to chill.
2. Pour the peach purée into chilled champagne flutes, then gently add the Prosecco. Stir gently. Garnish with a sprig of mint.

✳ Add some cherry or raspberry juice for a 'blush' colour.

Amaretto, Catherine Style

Makes 1 ½ litres

Learning from the Sicilians, I decided to bottle my own amaretto for Christmas gifts a few years ago. I was delighted with the results and it's really versatile for cooking too.

300g sugar
375ml boiling water
500ml vodka
500ml brandy
2 tbsp almond extract

1. Bring the sugar and water to a boil in a large pot. Boil uncovered for 2 minutes, then remove from the heat and allow to cool for 30 minutes. Add the remaining ingredients and pour into sterilised bottles.
2. Store at room temperature for at least 1 week before taking a tipple.

✳ Try this recipe with any extract available, from cherry to anise. The brandy is for colour, similar to amaretto, so use only vodka for the clearer liqueurs.

Index